A FRACTION OF A POINT

A Fraction of a Point

A Gymnastics Dynasty on the Line

Nina Mandell

The Kent State University Press · *Kent, Ohio*

ISBN 978-1-60635-507-7 (paperback)
ISBN 978-1-63101-585-4 (epub)
Published in the United States of America

Cataloging information for this title is available at the Library of Congress.

To my dad

Contents

CHAPTER 1

It's Over

Sitting in the bleachers after her team's final event—the balance beam—at the 2022 Ohio high school state meet—longtime Brecksville-Broadview Heights assistant coach Leah Miko began to cry.

Leah, a thirty-year-old former gymnast with her long brown hair tied back into a ponytail, knew that the team's winning streak of eighteen consecutive state titles wasn't going to extend to a nineteenth.

The meet had been going fine—even well—until the balance beam event, the final of four events of the meet. Of the six gymnasts who had competed for Brecksville, three had fallen.

Some of those gymnasts fell multiple times. Falling off of the balance beam is like a quick-spreading infection. Once one person does it, it's in the next gymnast's head. Once they fall, it's in everyone's head. And that's when the beam, more than four feet above the ground, is an impossible bar to stay on. Gymnastics, like most things, takes a lot of skill. But at Brecksville-Broadview Heights, there's always been focus on the mental aspect too. It wasn't enough, though, for this moment when a legacy that started before each of the gymnasts was born was slipping away with each fall.

Freshman Avery Butler was up first. She went into the meet as an alternate and wasn't expecting to compete, but she performed well on warmups—better than the gymnasts slated to compete—and so she was put in first in the lineup. Her mom, Jocelyn, looked down from the parents' section surprised that her daughter was up. "What is going on?" she asked, suddenly feeling a wave of stress. Jocelyn's stomach took another turn as she looked down and saw her daughter fall off the beam.

But it should have been fine. There were five Brecksville gymnasts to go.

Senior Erin Delahunty was up second. This one should have been an easy good score. Erin had been here three times before. She should have been confident in her last postseason event.

But steps into her routine, she slipped.

Leah and Brecksville Broadview Heights head coach Maria Schneider tried not to show their reaction in front of the gymnasts. Instead, they switched sides. It was their superstition that when a gymnast performed badly, it was because they were positioned incorrectly. There was no actual reason to think that, but they had convinced themselves for years that this was true. So they switched. And they waited as the next gymnast began her routine.

Leah stared down at her shoes and listened and heard the distinct pause in the routine and soft thud on the floor of a fall.

It's against the rules to coach a gymnast during the middle of the event, so Maria and Leah just offered some encouraging words. But it didn't matter. Even if they could have coached more, there wasn't really much they could say. This wasn't a skill issue. It was mental.

They were falling short of a championship performance. And they knew they were in trouble.

"Now we know we have to count a fall in our score," Maria realized.

She looked over at Leah. Her hand was on her face.

Leah had started to panic. Despite Leah's efforts to hide it, senior Lindsay Kern knew it too. She had known Leah for years—before she was on the high school team, Leah was her coach at Gymnastics World, the club gym where she and the other Brecksville gymnasts grew up training since they were in the mom-and-me classes as preschoolers.

Lindsay was a little bit scared and mostly impressed by Leah when she first arrived at the gym when Lindsay was in middle school—Leah had recently graduated from Bowling Green, where she walked onto the Division I team. And in Brecksville, Leah was a gymnastics legend—she was the best gymnast in the state of Ohio in her senior year of high school and was part of four state title wins. But over the years that Leah coached Lindsay and the other now-upperclassmen, she became something of a big sister figure and someone she could joke around with—in addition to being their tough coach.

Lindsay also knew the team needed above a 9.1 average for four of the six gymnasts competing in the beam event to beat last year's meet score and secure an easy win, or above a 9.3 for their stretch goal of the best score in Brecksville history, and that they were falling well short of that. At the very least, it shouldn't have been difficult to at least match last year's score on the beam, which was a 9.1 average—five teams, after all, had scored above a 36 in the event the year before. But as she watched her teammates slip one after another, Lindsay knew that her coaches were concerned.

"Horrible body language," she thought.

But Lindsay was calm. Leah walked over to check in before she started her routine. "I'm good," she said. Then, in her last time competing as a Brecksville gymnast, she stayed on the beam. As she dismounted, she thought she crushed it. She was engulfed in hugs from her teammates and looked to the judge panel for her score.

In high school gymnastics, each team has six gymnasts compete in each event. Of those scores, the top four are counted to the team score. Lindsay's routine may have been one of her best. She, after all, stayed on the beam. But it wasn't good enough to help boost her team score to what they needed. It wasn't her fault. That would have been a tall task, mathematically, for anyone at that point.

In the stands, the parents sat together quietly, nervous. "What is going on?" Jocelyn wondered, concerned that so many experienced gymnasts had performed so badly.

The gymnasts, lined up together on the side, also began to worry. The beam performance was bad enough that it could threaten their meet lead. But Brecksville gymnasts are taught better than to show their stress. So as each gymnast went up, they lined up and cheered as loudly as they could for each teammate.

When it was over, they knew it was bad. They finished with a 35.125 on beam, which was well under last year's finish. There would be only three teams out of twelve that did worse by the time the meet concluded. Awful. They couldn't see Leah, but she was distraught.

"I'm not an emotional person at all," Leah said later. "I never cry in front of the girls, so I had to wait until they left the gym."

The principal of Brecksville and the superintendent and the athletic director huddled around her on the bleachers and tried to comfort her.

"You guys did your best," they told her. "You did your best."

But for Leah, the words were empty. She was so disappointed—in herself.

"The lineup was wrong," she thought. She knew it was wrong.

She and Maria weren't confident going into beam—it had plagued them for most of the season. So, in the back gym during warmups, they lined up the top balance beam performers for something called a "beam-off"—basically a mini competition to see who was looking the best in the moment.

It went against the coaches' strategy they used each year of taking the top six performers based on averages from the season's previous meets, as they had always done. That way was logical. It depended only on math. They struggled in beam all season, though, and with the meet close, they thought they needed to do something different. So instead, this time, they had gone on feeling.

And it was a disaster.

Leah wanted to win for her seniors, the girls she had coached in club gymnastics since they were little kids, so that they could go out on top. The gymnasts wanted to win for her—someone they never wanted to let down. And they all wanted to win for Maria, the head coach, and her parents—Joan and the late Ron Ganim, who turned the program at Brecksville-Broadview Heights into a legendary one and had been a large influence on their community for decades and all of their lives since most were little kids.

And most of all, they didn't want to be the team that ended the streak.

. . .

The state meet was held at Hilliard Bradley High School outside of Columbus, Ohio. There are two gyms—the competition gym and the auxiliary gym. In the competition gym, which would be a basketball court on an ordinary day, there's a barrier surrounding the competition area and the parents and other fans watched from bleacher seating that looked down onto the floor. It felt like a high-pressure fishbowl.

The Brecksville-Broadview Heights parents huddled together. Their unofficial job was to keep tabs on the other teams throughout the meet. There's no scoreboard on the wall at the meet and four gymnasts competed in different events simultaneously throughout the day, so the gymnasts often had only a vague idea of where they were in the standings—and even if they've managed to piece it together, nothing was certain. At this meet, the parents were keeping an eye on the teams that they thought were likely to come the closest based on what they knew about them coming into the meet—Hudson, Magnificat, Kenston, Brunswick.

But the whole day wasn't going as they thought. "We need to keep an eye on Medina," a school in the southern suburbs of Cleveland, the scorekeeping parents realized as the gymnasts reached their final events.

They watched helplessly from the bleachers as Brecksville gymnast after Brecksville gymnast fell during the beam routine and saw the muted disappointment on their daughters' faces. They even caught the tears as they began to flow when the gymnasts walked into the back room. But they had to stay in the raised bleachers and wait for it to be over.

The only thing they could do was track the other teams. And doing the unofficial math, the parents watching knew that it was possible for Medina to overtake them for the state title if they performed well in their final event.

They knew it would take four Medina gymnasts scoring very well on uneven bars or better to do it if their math was correct.

But it was possible. It was definitely possible.

. . .

The Brecksville gymnasts sat quietly as they thought about what had just happened. They knew it was possible that they would go down in history as the team that broke the streak. That meant no trophies to add to the collection. No banner raised in the gym in their honor to be added to the already vast collection. No trip to be honored by the Brecksville City Council. No trip to be honored by the Broadview Heights City Council. Their place in the history books would be the first Brecksville-Broadview Heights team that lost in the state meet since before they were even born.

"It's going to be close," the team's matriarch, Joan Ganim, told them as they filed in.

They quietly texted their parents looking for score updates and sat on the floor, talking quietly in groups with their bags surrounding them. They watched, eyes welling up again, as the Medina High School team returned to the back gym, excited after their last event. And they had cupcakes.

Junior Ella Shaheen felt herself panicking as she looked over. "Oh my god," she thought. "Why would they have cupcakes unless it was to celebrate that they won states?"

Until that moment, she had had many happy moments as a member of the Brecksville-Broadview Heights team. Two state titles, her freshman and sophomore year. The smaller moments, the team dinners before each meet, the celebrations after states in the past. When the Brecksville-Broadview Heights gymnastics team walked into the room at high school meets, there's an air around them. Everyone knew who they were. They're intimidating. They're disciplined. They're perfectly coordinated from their matching ribbons to their red Crocs. They're the team that had held the state title out of reach for nearly two decades.

And in the back gym, Ella and those previously untouchable gymnasts were sure it was all over.

. . .

Brecksville-Broadview Heights won its first state title in 1994, when Maria was away at college and the team was coached by her parents, Ron and Joan Ganim.

Joan and Ron met in college at Kent State nearly three decades earlier. Joan, a college gymnast, was looking for a way to the school homecoming dance and needed a date. She asked a friend for help. He went to his fraternity house and said loudly to whoever could hear: "Anyone want to go on a date with a gymnast?"

Ron Ganim looked up. "I'll do it," he said. After getting Joan's dorm information, he went to the lobby of her dorm to meet her after her gymnastics practice.

"Bill said you wanna go to homecoming," he told her. "Would you wanna go with me?'

She was immediately smitten. He reminded her of something from home.

It was a date. Shortly after, the two were inseparable.

Being inseparable meant that Ron began to hang around gymnastics practice to the annoyance of the Kent State coach Rudy Bachna. Bachna told Ron, who had been a football player until an injury derailed his career a year earlier, that he could either try out for the team or be a coach.

So Ron gave it his best. He tried to vault. And in the immediate aftermath (it went badly), he chose coaching. It proved to be valuable time spent—he picked up enough about the sport to understand how to coach it and he learned how to run a practice. He graduated from college and Joan followed the year later. Sitting in a house that Joan rented with her sister, Ron proposed and the two settled in Brecksville, both working as teachers. Joan started coaching the Brecksville High School gymnastics team, then just a club team. She gave birth to Maria, and went back to teaching. Then, with only a few weeks left in the school year, she learned she was pregnant with Greg. She told the school's principal the good news to let him know that she would need to take time off the next school year.

Instead, she learned that day, a young mom sitting in her principal's office, that her teaching career was over.

"Mothers," the school principal told her, "need to be home with their children."

Her contract, she learned that day, would not be renewed the next year.

Joan was heartbroken. But she made no plans to stay at home.

Instead, using a bit of money from her parents, she and Ron founded Gymnastics World, one of the first private club gymnastics gyms in the region. She remained bitter at being forced out of her job in the school district, but when Maria decided to compete for Brecksville in high school fourteen years later, Joan and Ron returned as coaches and won their first state title in 1994.

Their second state title came in 2000, when Brecksville beat then four-time defending champions Rocky River Magnificat (which was better known as Magnificat) by .025 points. In 2004, the Bees won a third state title and hadn't lost one since.

Their title run produced memorable moments like when Alecia Farina, who went on to compete for the University of Maryland's gymnastics team, posted the first perfect 10 in OHSSAA history in 2015. There are championship banners that cover the wall of the Brecksville High School gym, leaving other coaches to grumble (more out of friendly jealousy than malice) that they'd like some room made for any they may win. A trophy case dedicated to Ron Ganim, who remained a teacher and football coach at Brecksville-Broadview Heights schools after his wife was let go, filled with gymnastics trophies and plaques welcomed visitors into the hallway at the high school.

The Ganims were beloved figures in Brecksville and inspired fierce loyalty from their current and former gymnasts. Many of them, including Leah, spent a large portion of their childhoods at Gymnastics World training. Leah thought of them as family. "She throws birthday parties for me," she said of Joan. "We go out to dinner all of the time."

Leah was hooked on gymnastics since her mom first brought her to Gym World on the recommendation of a friend when she was in preschool. Gymnastics quickly became her life and she competed for the high school as part of four of the state titles, some of them as close if not closer than this one. Four years after her fourth state title, she returned after college to Cleveland and immediately started coaching at Gymnastics World and her old high school and began her teaching career at another school. "I just wanted to be part of the legacy that I was a part of as a gymnast and continue it," she said. "I was one of the few (of former Brecksville gymnasts) that this was my whole life."

Everyone in the Brecksville program accepted that it was logical that the high school state title streak, like all sports streaks, would end one day. And that, every coach and adult around the program, insisted out loud, would just be that and the world would go on and they would try again next year.

It seemed like the right thing to say.

They never wanted to put too much pressure on the gymnasts. But that hadn't stopped them from putting pressure on themselves.

When Maria took over the program from her mom as the head coach in 2019, she often felt nauseous and envisioned what was happening at the 2022 state meet many times. She was sure she was going to lose the state title and find herself in the headlines on ESPN or highlighted on *The Ellen Show* for being the coach who ruined her parents' legacy. In her head was a glaring photo of herself with some sort of story about how she was the coach that ended a historic streak. The disapproving audience would boo. Her family, she thought, would be so embarrassed.

The gymnasts knew the stakes too, even as the adults around them tried to shield them from the pressure.

"People would notice more if we lost than if we won," Erin said. "Someone's going to mess up eventually, you just don't want to be the class that does it."

That was something Leah and Maria desperately did not want to face, as they crept out to watch the Medina team compete after Brecksville's disaster on the beam.

. . .

While there's no official scoreboard or way to quickly know how a team is doing throughout the meet, Leah and Maria had their ways. In addition to the intel from the parents, they swapped scores with other high school coaches, speaking quietly in passing between events, so they knew where they stood.

So, as the Brecksville coaches sat in the bleachers watching Medina, that's how Leah and Maria knew Medina would have to pull off the best bars score of the meet, a 38 (which would be 1.175 points higher than Brecksville's meet-high score). But Medina was a good team, and they knew it was certainly in the realm of possibility for it to happen for them or for their math to be off and the meet to be closer than they were counting.

After all, this was the state meet.

So they waited. And they watched as the first Medina gymnast competed. It was good, but not in the mid-9s. And then the second. Same result. By the third Medina gymnast's routine's score was announced, Leah did the math again in her head and allowed herself to start to breathe again. "They'd have to get a 9.9 on their last three to come close to us," she thought.

She relaxed. The streak was safe.

She took a big deep breath and looked at Maria.

Then, they started to cry again.

"Well, she was crying," Leah said later, insisting she had shed a single tear. "We just knew."

In past years, Leah and Maria would have rushed back to tell the gymnasts the good news. They were state champions.

But this time, they paused.

The coaches wanted them—especially the underclassmen—to remember this feeling of the stomach knot-inducing anxiety of failure. She wanted to remind them that they didn't live up to the standards that she had set for them and that they had set for themselves. "I just really wanted to let it marinate with them," Leah said.

• • •

Even without their coaches coming back with the good news, for the Brecksville gymnasts waiting in the auxiliary gym, there was also a sense of relief filtering through.

A kind Medina gymnast let Ella know that the cupcakes had been just to celebrate that they had made it to the state meet. Not that they had won.

Texts began to come in from the gymnasts' parents, hitting their phones as they scrolled through TikTok, that the streak was safe.

But no one wanted to celebrate early.

Leaving the team waiting in anticipation was the same thing Joan and Maria had done in the two years when Leah was a gymnast in high school and the state meets were really close.

Leah, who remembered those days when she was the one competing, wanted to make sure they got the message she did when she was in school.

"I think this was a year that with how hard they worked all season long, they didn't know that this was possible," Leah said. "And it did, in the blink of an eye, go south real quick."

So even though they had loosened a bit, the knots still sat in the stomachs of the Brecksville gymnasts as they filed back into the main gym for the awards ceremony and sat in a group on the gym floor, their parents still watching from the bleachers.

First, came awards for coach of the year and assistant coach of the year. They knew coming into the meet that Leah was going to win assistant coach of the year, so the gymnasts' parents had fatheads—large cutouts of her face—ready for their daughters. The gymnasts pulled them out of their shirts and waved them enthusiastically in the air as Leah walked to the stage.

Then, it was time to announce the runners-up.

The gymnasts gathered around in a circle and listened. In third place, they heard, was Kenston. Then, in second place, came Medina with a score of 145.025. The Brecksville gymnasts started to smile. They had won. They were state champions. "We all were so happy," senior Jenny Bandsuh said. "Despite that horrible beam day, we made it happen."

When their name was announced next, they all started cheering.

A few hours later, on the team's TikTok, they posted a video with the trend of a voiceover from the rapper Kanye West saying, "Everybody wants to know what I would do if I didn't win?" The camera then panned out to the gymnasts in their matching T-shirts with the trophy held high. "Luckily," the voiceover continued, "we'll never know."

They had won nineteen years in a row.

On the bus ride back to the hotel, it was a party. They blasted Beyoncé. They annoyed the bus driver. They didn't care.

The streak was alive. They had pulled it off.

In the front two seats, their coaches were already worrying about next year.

. . .

For Leah and Maria, making the team wait to hear the results wasn't just about the 2022 meet.

The coaches especially needed the underclassmen to understand what had happened in the 2022 meet to hammer home the point about what a big undertaking it would be next year when they go for their twentieth consecutive title. The team was losing its top three all-around contributors in a sport that needs to count four scores each event—so losing three quarters of their combined average counted scores. They didn't have a superstar gymnast they could count on to always bring up the team's average. Instead, they had eight freshmen coming in, none of whom were obvious stars. It could be their hardest year yet.

Hours after keeping the streak alive for one more year, it was all Leah and Maria could think about on the bus ride back to the hotel. Maria's mom, Joan, tried to get them to stop looking ahead and enjoy the moment they were in. "Just stop it," she told them. "You're going to be fine."

But it didn't help.

"I don't know about these incoming freshmen," Maria said. "They're not level 9 or 10 gymnasts, but they're good high school gymnasts.

"It should be interesting."

. . .

The next day, some of the gymnasts competed in the individual competition at the state meet. Gianna Ravagnani, a freshman, tied with Erin, a senior for first in the vault. Erin came in third in all-around, followed by Gianna in fourth. Jenny came in seventh. Then they all boarded the bus and headed back to Brecksville.

Leah was exhausted. She headed home to her house in the trendy Tremont area of Cleveland, a twenty-minute drive from Brecksville. She was so exhausted that she slept through when a little after midnight, a group of teenage girls used a trash can to climb onto her roof.

The next day, Leah looked at her security camera footage and sighed.

The gymnasts had crammed into the upperclassmen's cars and, trailed by Ella's dad, Matt Shaheen, had driven down to her house, armed with rolls of toilet paper.

In the video caught by Leah's security camera and posted to the Brecksville gymnastics TikTok, five gymnasts stood on the roof, dressed in all black. They did a synchronized dance and kicked a roll of toilet paper as a Kendrick Lamar song played behind them. "One last time pt. 2 on the roof #winditup #statechamps #fyp #teepee," they wrote in the caption.

Leah shouldn't have been surprised.

Toilet papering was a time-honored tradition for the Brecksville Bees.

It started even before Leah competed for the Bees when she was in high school. In her four years in high school, she spent her Saturday night following the state meet in her teammates' cars with rolls of toilet paper as well.

The tradition was that following the state title meet, the Bees went to one of the gymnasts' houses (this year it was Ella's), braided their hair, dressed in all black, and toilet papered a select list of homes. By recent tradition, it was the wrestling team (when Leah competed for the team it was other Brecksville sports teams)—they had their state meet that Saturday and weren't home yet. In recent years, the tradition also expanded to include some of the gymnastics coaches' houses, incoming freshmen, and more.

Leah was not amused.

The gymnasts thought it was hilarious.

And then, to top off the night, they were thrilled to have met Leah's friendly neighbor and her neighbor's pet.

"Skunky," Ella explained later. "Her pet skunk."

Leah walked outside the next morning and sighed at the toilet paper covering her roof and the side of her house.

As she picked it off the roof begrudgingly, she started to formulate a plan on how to convince the team that she moved to an unknown address before the end of next year's season so they wouldn't find her house for the prank.

. . .

It was August, still months before the 2022–23 season started and five months after the 2022 state title win. Leah stood at Gym World at a club practice, wearing her usual coaching uniform: black workout pants and a T-shirt, with her long curly brown hair pulled back in a ponytail. She watched her group of club gymnasts complete their warmup drills and tried to stop her mind from wandering. Two of the gymnasts in the club practice were Brecksville gymnasts, but the rest competed for other area schools—Padua, Strongsville, Magnificat, and more. It was a weird reality of the Ohio gymnastics scene really—she was doing her best to coach the gymnasts at Gym World who could potentially upset her high school team—her alma mater and the thing that drove her to near madness daily—in the next state meet. And while she was coaching the club gymnasts, often her mind kept wandering to that high school team. She had the same problem when she was driving to and from school or was at one of her other jobs—she also worked as a bartender—and mostly, it was the worst before she went to sleep at night.

Leah couldn't stop her mind from thinking about the hurdles facing the Brecksville-Broadview Heights team the next season. The lack of depth and known talent on the upcoming season roster was the thing that haunted her when she was not rethinking her strategy and where it almost went wrong with the last team. It had been months, but she couldn't get it out of her head.

She thought about how she was going to change her coaching style next season. She was going to see the incoming wave of tension or pressure at the start of the season and balance it out with upbeat positivity and calmness. That, she thought, was what went wrong at the state meet. "I've learned in my coaching career that every group of athletes is so different and this group cannot be serious," she said. "If they're serious about it, then they really fall apart. So they almost need to have this joking, more relaxed manner. And that was really hard for me as a coach because that's not how I grew up.

"I was very serious. I was very type A—hey, we need to focus, we need to dial in. So that was an adjustment for me."

The group had also dealt with something unprecedented—two years of COVID-19 that changed their lives and what the sport looked like. The 2021 meet, the year before, everyone who wasn't competing watched from the hotel on a live feed instead of in the gym with their teammates. Gymnasts who were accustomed to their teammates standing on the sidelines and supporting them with cheers, encouragement, and just familiar faces, were instead greeted with the unfamiliar and unsupportive faces of masked officials. Their parents also watched from the lobby of the hotel, gathered around a single TV. It was the only way to keep the sport going. So in 2022, Leah was trying mostly to remind them of what gymnastics was supposed to be. And why they all loved their high school team experience. But then when the pressure of the last event at the state meet came, Leah thought that's when the mood was out of her control and there was nothing she could do to bring it back. It got too serious.

"I didn't know how to coach that because I've been coaching them to be silly and be relaxed, but still have enough balance of focus. But they had a lot less pressure when they were silly. And I feel that they felt pressure because we had a goal of hitting 150 points as a team to break the state record. And we were on track to do that after the third event. A beam score that we've hit many times before."

Later that night after the team portion of the state meet, when she was preparing the gymnasts for the individual meet the next day, Leah tried to put it in perspective. But she found that the maddening thing in the perspective was that sometimes, things that are supposed to be easy end up being hard. And out of your control. Figuring out how to coach out of that—that was what she had to conquer in the upcoming season.

"There's some days where the cards just weren't in our favor," she had told her team as they sat at the hotel in Columbus that Friday night after the team portion of the state meet, "and, you know, that beam wasn't in our favor."

Even knowing that it was just a bad day on the beam and the team had actually ended up winning by a good margin, the other thing that kept her up at night was how she was going to avoid coaching mistakes this season. A bad day on beam with three experienced seniors leading the pack wasn't anything compared to the out-of-her-control factors heading into the team's run at a twentieth consecutive title. When she was done thinking about the 2022 state meet, Leah often ticked through the freshmen coming through whom she knew from club gymnastics and tried to place them in lineups in her head. She thought about the two seniors—Delaney Evans and Ella—and what kind of leaders they would be. She thought about junior Lea Haverdill coming back from an injury that had kept her sidelined for her sophomore year. She thought about the outgoing freshmen, Gianna (GG), Rachel Kelly, and Avery and if a year of experience at the state meet was going to make it easier enough next season to ignore the pressure. She wondered if incoming junior Jeanne Winzen's back would be healthy enough for her to make an impact. She wondered what other teams were going to come back with as they tried to knock down the ever-defending champions.

Leah opened each season by giving a speech to the team. She talked about how it's a team sport and they compete for their team. It's not club gymnastics, where they're competing for themselves. She talked about how she doesn't care if you fall off the beam, she cares about if you are cheering for your teammates as they compete after you.

Her talk for the next season would include one more piece of advice.

"We don't have as much talent as we've had in years past," she said. "We don't have that star athlete. We don't even have two mediocre athletes; we have a very young team with eight freshmen coming in.

"But hard work is something that we'll all have."

Standing at Gym World as she called out drills for her club practice, she went through the events of the mistakes made in the state meet and last season again. She would confidently reiterate her points about working hard and being a good team player.

Inwardly, she didn't know. She hoped hard work would be enough.

CHAPTER 2

Gym World

Brecksville and Broadview Heights, the two towns whose students went to Brecksville-Broadview Heights High School, were leafy suburbs on the west side of Cleveland, about twenty minutes from the airport and the same from downtown Cleveland. Both towns were known as a nice place to raise kids, almost "a bubble" as one gymnast described it and a place filled with green space and was close enough to commute to the Cleveland Clinic, the well-respected medical center that occupied a large portion of the city, or any of the other major employers in the area.

The main street of Brecksville, Brecksville Road, led to one of the neighboring suburbs, Independence, and a portion of it was renamed in 2016 to honor the Cleveland Cavaliers' NBA championship. (Their practice facility was also in Independence before it moved downtown. In 2023, the former Cleveland Cavaliers player Kevin Love gave a shout-out to Brecksville shortly after he left the team to play for Miami but was most likely referring to Brecksville Road in Independence.)

In 2021, AJ Ganim, the youngest of the Ganim siblings, won a spot on the Brecksville City Council. He was one of three newcomers that year and received 19 percent of the vote, with 2,507 in his favor. He was the second-place finisher and under Brecksville's charter, the top three vote-getters were voted in for a four-year term. (The fourth-place candidate served a two-year term before coming up for reelection.) Annually, the Brecksville-Broadview Heights gymnastics team was honored by the City Council for winning the state title.

When AJ's parents, Ron and Joan, moved there after college, Joan had thought it seemed like a step up from Independence, where she had grown up and Parma, another further west-side working-class suburb about fifteen minutes from Brecksville, where Ron had grown up. "It was one of the ritzier suburbs," she said of Brecksville.

On the other side of the 71 freeway from Brecksville is Broadview Heights, where to get to Gym World, you drove past the shopping center with the Wild Eagle Steak and Saloon restaurant and turned left onto a treelined street.

Tucked into the back of a parking lot that's easy to miss right before the neighborhood turned residential was the current location of Gymnastics World Broadview Heights, one of the three branches of Gymnastics World owned by the Ganim family.

Gym World, as most people referred to it, was the private gym that trained most of the Brecksville-Broadview Heights gymnasts and was fully credited for a large role in the state win streak and all of the other successes. As Shawn Miko, Leah's older brother, once put it, "They're a factory for putting out successful high school gymnasts."

Now a towering partner in the community, Gym World began for a simple reason. The Ganims needed money.

Joan had been a teacher since she graduated from Kent State and she loved it. She was good at it. So, on the days after she was fired, she said goodbye to her husband before he drove to school for his job while she stayed home. She felt the tears well up.

"I loved what I was doing. I mean, I was teaching health and physical education at the junior-high level, and then I was coaching besides, so I enjoyed what I was doing, and all of a sudden now that first day of school, whenever my husband went to school and the buses were driving, I cried," she said.

Of course she loved getting to spend time with her children. She loved them deeply. But she wanted to work. And, financially, she needed to—they had gone from living on two teaching salaries to one when her contract wasn't renewed, and they had added expenses with a new baby.

"We had to do something," she said.

She and Ron came up with a plan. It was one that would make her longtime dreams come true and, hopefully, put the family in a better financial position.

Joan's first love was dancing. She had been a dancer and acrobat her entire life before she discovered gymnastics as a student at Kent

State when she was looking for a way to get involved in campus life. It had always been her dream to open a dance studio.

She technically had already operated one. As a teenager, she held dance classes for the neighborhood kids in her basement, charging 25 cents each. She'd teach tap and tumbling.

The Ganims considered business options. Though Joan had dreamed of a dance studio, private gymnastics studios were a new but up-and-coming concept with less competition and with a better potential customer base. Joan coached the school district's gymnastics club teams as part of her teaching job, and she and Ron ran clinics in the summer. People already knew that she was a good coach.

The Ganims went to Joan's parents with their business plan, and they gave them enough cash to help get them off the ground.

Ron's first move, once he and Joan decided their plan, was to walk down to the house two doors down from where they lived. That's where he found Mike Helus, a former Brecksville gymnast and their neighbor. Mike had a few important qualities—he had helped them coach previously at camps that they put on for local kids, and he was one of those guys who could fix anything. He was changing the oil in his car when Ron walked up and asked what he was up to.

"I said, 'I'm changing the oil on my car,'" Mike remembered. "And he said, 'You could do that?' I go 'Yeah yeah. You just have to take the old oil out and put the new stuff in.'"

Ron considered this for a moment, impressed.

"He said, 'Well, whenever you get the chance, Joan has a question she wants to ask you,'" Mike remembered. "She has some idea she wants to get a small private gymnastics school going.'" They were aiming, Ron said, for about twenty-five to fifty customers to start. They thought with Mike's background in gymnastics and his general ability to solve problems, he would be perfect.

It was potentially a crazy idea. Mike said he was in. Next on the list, the group needed to find a lease. They looked at small spaces, a place that was undeveloped under a building, basements, and more. "There was the basement that was a dark dungeon, and we decided not to stay there," Mike remembered.

They chose a space that was part of a warehouse where they were given space for a gym floor and an office.

As they were signing the lease, the landlord stopped the group to express his concerns. "Are you sure you want to sign this?" he asked. "Because if you do, you're going to owe me rent for the next three years."

The landlord's doubt wasn't totally unfounded as Greg Ganim, the son whose birth made Joan lose her job, pointed out. It was a different time from the current day when parents signed their kids up for an overscheduled amount of recreational and higher-end sports. "In the 1970s, no one paid for sports," Greg pointed out. "You went to school and you played football, or you played basketball, or you were a cheerleader. And so when gymnastics came along and they questioned, why would someone pay you when they could do it for free? And so that's why everyone thought they were crazy. I think they just kind of saw the future that this is how it's going to be. So they went for it."

On that day signing the lease, Joan, Ron, and Mike nodded when the skeptical landlord asked if they were sure. They were going to make this work. The Ganims put their advertisements in the local newspaper and the phonebook. And they relied on word-of-mouth. When Gym World opened in September 1975, dozens of eager kids—and their parents looking for an outlet for their energy with coaches who already had a good reputation for being positive and trusted teachers—poured in over the opening months, far surpassing their expectations.

"People just started dribbling in," Joan said. "We were hoping for fifty to sixty kids and we had a hundred."

Joan, with two small children at the time, taught all the classes—the rec classes, the little kid classes, the adult classes. The second year, Mike helped out with the boys' classes and Joan added a competitive team. "We literally had a pole in the middle of our floor area," Joan laughed. "We danced around it."

As the gym grew, they moved to a space nearly twice as big in 1978 and by 1985, they built their own facility in Broadview Heights, a one-story building, later adding a loft space above the workout space used for meetings and classes and a hallway full of offices. The gym space was lined with trophies that covered the edges of the ceiling surrounding the workout space (they had to clean them to get the dust off a few times a year). Banners hung down throughout. And in the hallway outside the gym, there were photos of former Gym World gymnasts in their college uniforms or state champion teams from the last decade.

In 2014, they added Gym World Twinsburg to the family, and AJ ran a cheerleading gym that's in the Gym World family too.

In the end, Gym World ended up changing the trajectory of their family, all of whom were involved in the business as adults. Greg remembered a conversation he had with his mom about why they had started the gym in the first place. Their goals, he learned, were more than just making a place for kids to learn the sport. "Their number-one reason was to just take care of their family, make sure that their family had everything," he said. "And I said, well check, you did that. Good job. And then from there it grew."

Their business plan for the gym also quickly became different from those of many of the private gymnastics clubs that existed at the time. Most aimed only to train gymnasts who could compete at a high level or even make the Olympics. The other clubs often had a business model that was based on the success of their young kids and teenagers.

In one meet in the early days of Gym World, Joan and Ron watched a coach from another gym berate a young gymnast at a regional meet. Ron stepped in and calmly helped the teenager. Later, when Ron spoke to the girl's father, he was taken aback. The man thanked him for helping and Ron asked why he would let someone speak to his daughter that way. Decades later, Joan remained chilled by his response.

"He's supposed to be the best," the father said of the coach.

That type of coaching was common at the time, though—especially for gymnasts who wanted to make it to the Olympics or compete at any sort of high level—to put up with horrific abuses.

It was a culture that produced eating disorders in gymnasts who worried about being too fat, which encouraged gymnasts to fight through devastating injuries to compete. It was a culture on the national level that would leave USA Gymnastics heroes cheered on by Americans during the Olympics to tell stories decades later of the emotional, physical, and sexual abuse they suffered through in the name of achieving their dreams—and how those experiences sullied all of it. And it was one that would leave talented gymnasts behind from the top levels with their confidence crushed and their bodies injured. And the acceptance of that type of coaching sometimes filtered down to gyms across the country that were hoping to find the gymnast who would put them on the map.

Watching that coach and coaches like him who berated young gymnasts, the Ganins knew they didn't want to be part of that gymnastics culture. They wanted to be different and they expected their staff to have a positive impact on their gymnasts' lives, not depend on them for fame. Even in gyms where gymnasts were treated well, as early as elementary school, they're encouraged to fit their education around gymnastics and often be homeschooled instead of the other way around, where gymnastics fits into their education.

Joan and Ron decided then that their gym would be different. When parents come in with Olympic hopes for their children, the staff was quick to shut that down nicely. "We're not the place for that," they'd say.

"I'd never tell a kid no," said Greg, who became one of the co-owners of Gym World. "But I'll tell the parents, no, sorry, we don't do that. If you want to do that, there's other gyms in Texas or you can go to in Columbus. But I don't know. I think our brand of gymnastics is trying to get a kid to college, you know? Keep them happy, let them have an athlete-student balance in life. These kids that train for elite gymnastics, most of them, 99 percent of them come in in the morning and they do a workout, and then they do school and then they work out again.

"I think that's just a little too much. It's not, it's just not for us. It's just not our brand of gymnastics. We were just happy to be able to spread what we do best to more people is really what it came down to."

. . .

Dominique Moceanu, an Olympic gold medalist who at fourteen was the youngest gymnast to win a gold medal and was part of the "Magnificent Seven" in the 1996 Olympics, had retired from competing when she walked into Gym World in the early 2000s. She was there with her boyfriend at the time (who later became her husband), Mike Canales, an Ohio State star who had trained at Gym World in high school.

Speaking to *Cleveland Magazine* in 2003, the couple told the story of how they had met first at the US National Championships when Dominique was twelve. Mike was sixteen and they spoke a bit—Dominique had just won the junior division. They continued to see each other throughout the years sporadically, but it wasn't until 2001, when they were both retired, that they got to know each other as spectators at the national championships. Months later, Mike asked Dominique, according to the magazine, if she would be interested in potentially coaching at Gym World. It would also mean her moving from Houston to Cleveland to be closer to him.

As an Olympic hopeful, Dominique had trained in the environment that Ron and Joan were so determined to avoid. In interviews with HBO's *Real Sports, The Los Angeles Times,* and others since she retired, she accused then–USA Gymnastics coordinators Bela and Martha Karolyi of mentally and physically abusing her at a young age.

Moceanu spoke out about her treatment by the Karolyis, who also owned Karolyi Ranch, which was used as the Olympic training center, in interviews with HBO's *Real Sports* and *The Los Angeles Times* in 2008. In an interview with *The Los Angeles Times* that year, she said that Martha Karolyi had slammed her head into a phone when she was just fourteen years old.

"I never, ever objected to hard work," Moceanu told the newspaper at the time. "What I objected to was Martha grabbing me by the neck, shoving my face into the phone and telling me to call my parents when I hurt my neck in practice. I objected to being told to jump onto a scale in front of the 1995 world championship team, of being forced to do 16 uneven bars routines in a row by Martha.

"I was completely embarrassed by Bela in front of the 2000 national training team at camp. He completely belittled me and my weight, singled me out, and made me feel very small. It was unfair treatment. Martha's logic is so false but no one would listen to a 14-year-old. I was never allowed to speak out." In a 2021 interview with *The Daily Mail,* Moceanu said she was labeled "fat" by her coaches at the Olympic training center, who "restricted her food intake while subjecting her to physical and emotional abuse."

"Our coaches told us, 'Don't eat, you're fat,'" she told the newspaper. "That's not what you tell a prepubescent teen. It's so damaging. I was told to starve myself by my coaches, and any time I performed poorly, they said it was because I was fat."

. . .

Mike Helus remembered when Dominique walked into the doors of Gym World where Mike was training, and she quickly marveled at the atmosphere she saw. It was just so different from what she had been subjected to.

When looking back at it nearly twenty years later, Joan remembered Dominique saying that she wanted to get involved. "We just said sure," Joan laughed. "I guess that would be okay."

(In that 2003 article, Joan told *Cleveland Magazine* that the two spoke on the phone and at first they were a bit skeptical, wondering if Dominique's training background would be too intense but were quickly assured after watching her coach one weekend.)

Mike Helus remembered Ron responding in typical Ron fashion, unbothered by her star power. "He started her as an assistant coach," he said. For years, though, Dominique was mentioned in local articles as a Gym World coach. When the Bees won the title in 2007, one of the gymnasts, Kristy Ryan, was quick to point to her as a big reason for the moment.

"Dominique taught us respect for the sport, made us more disciplined," she told the *Cleveland Plain Dealer.* "But we could also relate to her as teenagers, too, because she's been through it all." Moceanu told the *Plain Dealer* that she was grateful "for the opportunity to help the team win its fourth consecutive state title, and understands the emotions the seniors are feeling better than most."

"After four years, all that hard work finally paid off, but just like that, it's over and time to move on," Moceanu told the newspaper. "I know they'll take the values, the respect, the discipline with them."

. . .

In 2017, nearly a decade after Moceanu publicly complained about her treatment in USA Gymnastics, Steve Penny, the USA Gymnastics president and CEO, resigned under pressure as the organization faced heavy criticism over its handling of allegations of sex abuse by local club coaches and US Olympic team doctor Larry Nassar. In 2018, Nassar was sentenced to up to 175 years in prison for sexually abusing dozens of young gymnasts, including some of USA Gymnastics' biggest stars. His sentencing came at the end of a seven-day hearing where more than 150 gymnasts testified about the abuse he subjected them to under the guise of medical care. That year, USA Gymnastics filed for bankruptcy, a move related to the hundreds of millions of dollars in lawsuits it faced from the sex abuse scandal.

Dozens of elite gymnasts spoke out about stories of training at the Karolyi Ranch that echoed the stories Moceanu told a decade earlier, of coaches blaming bad performances on eating too much, where medical care was subpar, and training was held in a place where they said conditions made it easier for Nassar to victimize them. They also spoke about the lack of investment and protection from the USOC and USA Gymnastics, even as they were winning gold medals at the Olympics. Gold medal gymnast Aly Raisman, who described to the *Washington Post* subpar food and medical care at the Karolyi Ranch, sued USA Gymnastics and the USOC in 2018. She alleged the organizations "willfully" didn't "implement appropriate safeguards" at the ranch and in other official team settings.

(The Karolyis denied wrongdoing and were never criminally charged. A district attorney who brought charges against Nassar said the Karolyis cooperated fully with the investigation, according to the *New York Times*.)

Karolyi Ranch was closed in early 2018 after US gymnast Simone Biles expressed her disbelief on Twitter that it was still the base for US Olympic training. "It is impossibly difficult to relive these experiences and it breaks my heart even more to think that as I work towards my dream of competing in Tokyo 2020, I will have to continually return to the same training facility where I was abused," she wrote.

In 2021, USA Gymnastics and the US Olympic and Paralympic Committee settled with Nassar's victims for $380 million.

. . .

The same year the Karolyi Ranch closed, Moceanu, after spending years seeing a different way of coaching at Gym World, opened her own gym in Medina, a nearby suburb to Broadview Heights, with the motto "peace, strength, and balance," with the goal of "an inclusive, friendly and positive atmosphere."

. . .

For Maria, Greg, and AJ, having parents who owned Gym World meant a few things. First, they grew up in Gym World—they were all gymnasts for at least some portion of their lives. And second, many of their friends knew their parents not only as their parents but also as the owners of their gymnastics gym. Everyone's parents knew their parents, it seemed.

Gym World offered everything from toddler classes where parents joined to help spark an interest (or just get out some energy) through level 10 (the highest level) club coaching. Higher-level club gymnasts spent four to five days after school there.

In addition to the chance that someone would know their parents from Gym World, Ron was also a teacher at the school and a longtime football coach. So whenever the three tried to do anything against the rules, they felt like they were immediately caught by some parent who just happened to be right there. Ron was a larger-than-life teddy bear with glasses and an outsized personality that filled the room. Joan was petite, with a short haircut and was usually dressed in a sweat suit and sneakers. They were surrogate parents to dozens of gymnasts who came through the program. They socialized with a large group of friends in the area. Everyone knew them.

"I joke because I feel bad for these kids. People talk about how these kids can't get away with anything anymore because of social media. Somehow before social media was even invented, we were in that situation," Greg remembered. "I'll never forget eighth grade. I went to the mall. [My parents] never wanted me to go to the mall, right? That's what we did. Went to the mall and my friends all got to go . . . And so I snuck away and went to the mall. And like four people by Saturday morning had told them they saw me at the mall, you know, and I came into practice that Saturday morning and, and he's just like, 'You can't get away with anything, you know?'"

Ron was also the high school health teacher, which meant that he taught sex ed, at least when Greg was in high school. AJ was spared the embarrassment. "Yeah, so imagine, you were in 10th grade, you were 16 years old and you're already embarrassed if your parents talked to you about sex, but then," Greg remembered laughing, "he's telling all my friends about sex. But he made it so fun. You'd walk into his classroom and he would be wearing a diaphragm as a hat, or he would have a condom tree on his desk just to embarrass me."

He thought about that last sentence for a minute.

"Or that's what he did. I dunno if it was to embarrass me, that's what I felt like," Greg continued. "But he would throw condoms around the room at kids and he brought himself down to the level of a 16-year-old to talk about stuff. So a lot of times in my life I used to say, all right, dad enough. But I always knew I should listen to him, even though sometimes I told him I'm not listening. But of course I was."

For Joan and Ron, owning Gym World meant that in addition to being husband and wife, they became business partners, something that defined their marriage thereafter. "I mean, most people that were in the business with their husbands ended up in divorces," Joan said. "But I guess the two of us, we could argue about things, but we'd forget about them just as quickly, and we never held it inside."

. . .

Of the hundreds of children who went through Gym World every year, Joan hoped to give them a foundation for something, even if it wasn't gymnastics. "A lot of these kids will start out in gymnastics, but they're not gonna be gymnasts. You know, their bodies change. Some get tall, some don't really like it, so they tend to go to basketball or volleyball. Then there's others who mentally just don't like it or they become dancers. But the foundations and the fundamentals you get from the sport is so beneficial to them. Because gymnastics on the recreational side, it still teaches you body awareness and, and gives you some strength. I mean, you have to develop muscles to support yourself on the bars even in the rec programs," she said. "And so it helps them."

The time commitment, once gymnasts got to the competitive level, quickly became twenty to thirty hours a week, with hours of practice required after school and on weekends. The injuries could add up. It's expensive. Joan was fine with all of that. She just wanted Gym World to be a positive influence on the gymnasts' lives for however long they're there, even if they didn't make it through high school there. Parents also said the Ganims and club coaches were quick to be honest about a gymnast who wasn't going to make it to the next level, giving them the opportunity to cut their losses and try something else or at least a less-competitive path that might be a better fit.

But for all those who dropped out, a large core of gymnasts advanced every year.

And that was the core that was most important to Joan and Ron's legacy.

Because even if Gym World didn't become a feeder to the Olympics or even a guarantee of a college scholarship, it did become "a gymnast factory" for one team: the Brecksville-Broadview Heights High School team. And it was one of the gymnasts closest to them who brought them back to the school where Joan had been unceremoniously pushed out more than a decade before.

CHAPTER 3

Back to High School

Fourteen years after the start of Gym World, Maria Ganim made a decision. She told her parents that for her sophomore year at Brecksville-Broadview Heights High School, she wanted to stop competing for the Gym World club team and compete only on the high school gymnastics team.

Joan was concerned about the effect that quitting the club team would have on her daughter's dreams of being a college gymnast. But she and Ron agreed and Joan decided that meant one thing. Despite Joan's lingering feelings about how she was forced out of her job, she and Ron would return as the high school's gymnastics coaches. The school's administration had changed and they had been asking the Ganims to come back anyway—in fact, the team was already training at Gym World's facilities. When Maria decided to compete for the high school team, Joan knew it was time for her to come back and take over.

The reason was simple: She just wanted to spend more time with her daughter. "I knew it was the only way I would see her," she said.

There were a few rules that Joan insisted on. First, no one was cut. Everyone had a chance to contribute to the program, though not everyone would get a chance to compete in the state meet. She would try as much as possible to give everyone competition opportunities. "I don't care if you can't do a forward roll," she said. "You could be on the team."

What she was most strict about was that if the gymnasts wanted to be on the team—stars or not—they had to show up to practice or have a good reason why they weren't there. "If they don't show up, then they get kicked off. But if they want to show up to the practices and they're going to work and do the things we ask them, they can be on the team."

She also insisted that there be a pathway for the gymnasts to get varsity letters—that stemmed from her own frustration with AJ, her youngest son's experience in football at Brecksville. "He had to wait until he was a senior to get this letter," Joan remembered. "And I decided I will never let that happen to my gymnasts, to anybody. It's not fair."

Some years they would have enough gymnasts to field three lineups at a meet if it had been allowed, which meant that dozens of gymnasts were showing up for hours of practice without a chance to ever have the glory of competing in the state meet—or sometimes any meet at all.

"Our goal is to get as many kids as we can to be able to compete at the state meet at some point," said Maria, whose last name changed to Schneider when she got married. "And the years where we had thirty kids, they knew that it wasn't even a chance. When there were thirty kids, we had three squads, but now the squads have been smaller, and so over the years we've been able to get more in."

Even with a smaller roster, it still wasn't a guarantee, though, that a Brecksville gymnast would ever make it to the state meet. As much as the Ganims stressed participation, they were there to win—if that's what the gymnasts decided they wanted. They left it to them to decide their goal each year. Despite that, some gymnasts who went through the program came back to complain in later years that they thought they should have gotten a spot.

They're rare. But those conversations stuck with Maria and Joan.

In some years, when their team was in a solid place at the state meet, they could make magic happen. Maria smiled when she talked about the time they were able to put a gymnast with special needs, Marina Hearns, in the lineup for the floor exercise. It was her senior year and she was a team captain. "She gave it her all, every time she went out on the floor and we were able to put her out there on that floor and to have the whole gym watch her."

It was her time to shine. And the entire audience—a group of people who rarely cheered for Brecksville gymnasts—went nuts. It was the state meet, so three other events were going on around her. But the crowd turned their attention to Marina and enthusiastically rooted for her, cheering on her every move.

"They clapped and she got a standing ovation," Maria added. "It was cool. It was really neat."

Joan and Ron were also the rare club gym owners who even encouraged—or allowed—their gymnasts to participate in high school. An important key to Brecksville's success was Gym World's policy on competing in high school—something that for the majority of Brecksville's reign was often frowned upon or not allowed by club gyms around the state. Many club coaches saw high school gymnastics as a distraction from their goals of helping their gymnasts compete in college or at a higher level or even the club state, regional, and national meets.

Ron and Joan believed that high school gymnastics gave gymnasts the chance to have fun and show their friends what they were working on for the hours and hours they spent in the gym. High school gymnastics offered a more fun atmosphere—it's a team sport so the pressure wasn't all on one person and it was up to everyone to contribute to a positive and encouraging atmosphere. Where club gymnastics didn't often have team dinners or game day traditions, high school gymnastics was able to provide some of what's often the most memorable moments in team sports. "The kids had something to look forward to when they got to high school," Maria said. And that, more than anything, was supposed to be the point.

The gymnastics team at Brecksville-Broadview Heights went from a club sport to a varsity one during Joan and Ron's first time as the head of the program in the 1970s. When they came back, Worthington, North Olmstead, and Cincinnati Turpin were the blueblood programs. Brecksville wasn't really in the conversation of top teams. In 1990, Rocky River Magnificat, a private all-girls school about twenty minutes from Brecksville, began its reign in Ohio gymnastics. And they set the bar each year that Brecksville tried to reach with their gymnasts during Joan and Ron's first years back.

Many of Magnificat's gymnasts trained at Great Lakes Gymnastics, another private gym in the area co-owned by Magnificat coach Joe Gura (Great Lakes opened in the further west Avon Lake suburb in 1978, three years after Gym World). Like the Brecksville team, their gymnasts were among the few club gymnasts allowed to participate in high school. Gura, also a Kent State graduate, and his gymnasts won each year from 1990 to 1993.

Though Maria enjoyed her time competing on the team, she never won the state title as a gymnast. She was away at college in 1994, when Brecksville—a team that had placed sixth in the state tournament the year before—won its first title, beating Magnificat (which finished second that year by 2.3 points). A (friendly) rivalry was born. But at least for the first decade, it was a bit one-sided with Magnificat dominating with the exception of the 1994 title.

It would be six years before Brecksville caught Magnificat again, winning the 2000 title by .025 points. Maria had returned from college where she was a walk-on on the Kent State team, and, following in the footsteps of her dad, became a health and physical education teacher at the middle school. She was an assistant coach for the high school team, the cool, younger coach who could relate to the gymnasts because she was so close to their age.

Even though it was at the beginning of her coaching career, it was that meet that crystallized a philosophy that keeps Maria up at night: A team was always a fraction of a point—whether that's a slip on the beam or a slightly off angle on vault or a missed step on floor or a fall on bars or something similar—away from a loss. Because for Brecksville to take the title over a team that had won eight of the last ten, that's what it took for them.

Their first state title win in 1994 came, at least by gymnastics standards, pretty handily. But it was the second state title, in 2000, that shaped Maria's understanding of the sport ever since. In state meets, each team competed in four events—uneven bars, vault, balance beam, and floor exercise. The order in which they competed varied. In 2000, Magnificat's last event was uneven bars. They completed the bars and their final score was 143.975, putting them in first place in the competition. Brecksville's final event, which happened to be after Magnificat's, was the floor exercise. Brecksville scored a 36.950 to win by a .025 of a point.

From then on, that was Maria's mantra. They were always a fraction of a point away from winning or losing the meet, which over the years became an even bigger possible disaster as the streak grew. Her coworkers at the middle school would hear her talking on the phone in the hall about it and could finish her sentence about being only a fraction of a point away from a loss. As an assistant coach, she quickly learned a different kind of pressure than she'd experienced as a gymnast. And as it grew, the team's state title streak—and what went into it—became ingrained not only in Maria but in the people and community that surrounded her.

. . .

Four years later, Brecksville won its third state title and what would be the first in its dominant state win streak, beating Magnificat. That year was also the start of the careers of the class of 2007, led by Christina Lenny, Victoria Moskalow, and Christine Abou-Mitri, who all went on to compete for Kent State after high school, just like Joan and Maria. The Brecksville team won again during that trio's sophomore year by a healthy margin of 1.55 points (two in a row) and junior year by more than 3 points (third in a row).

Then, in her senior year, Christina—known as "Lenny"—won the all-around on individual day—a feat, that as Cleveland.com noted at the time, came after being woken up for a 2:30 A.M. fire alarm set off by another hotel guest smoking a cigarette, according to the report. The day before, on team day, Brecksville won the state title that year by more than 6 points over the second-place finisher, Magnificat—a large margin. If it was a basketball or football game, it would have been called a blowout. "The seniors called themselves the Magnificent Seven," Maria remembered, a nod to the 1996 Summer Olympics team that featured Amy Chow, Amanda Borden, Dominique Dawes, Shannon Miller, Dominique Moceanu, Jaycie Phelps, and Kerri Strug. It was Brecksville's fourth straight title—the team's seniors that year became the first class to win each of their four years in high school.

When that group of seniors graduated, Brecksville lost some dependable talent and a difference-maker in Christina, who went on to be inducted into the Kent State Athletics Hall of Fame in 2022, but there was still a deep bench behind them, including Leah Miko, who was a freshman on the 2007 title team. Throughout the years, sometimes the wins seemed easy—Brecksville often had a superstar or two who were just far above any other high school gymnast in the state—or at least one or two gymnasts who went on to compete in college each year. And in 2013, there was no bigger star at Gym World than Alecia Farina.

Alecia began gymnastics at Gym World before she could remember. "My mom likes to tell me that she put me in gymnastics because I had so much energy and I would flip off the couch. You know, pretty much every other gymnast's reasoning why they started gymnastics for the most part," she said. She instantly loved gymnastics—and was good at it. By middle school, she was spending thirty hours a week at Gym World training with the competitive team. "I tried other sports like softball and dancing and things like that and I think it just wasn't enough of a challenge for me," she said. "One of the things about gymnastics is no matter how many hours you train each week, each day, there's always something new to learn. So I think that was the biggest thing for me was once I got a skill, I said okay, what's the next thing I can do?"

Alecia also saw the Ganims often at home from her window. When she was a kid, her family bought the house right behind them. They shared a backyard.

"At first I kind of thought it was weird because I thought, 'Oh my God, what if I'm doing cartwheels in the backyard, in the grass and [Ron] yells at me or if I'm on my trampoline, is he going to say, 'Hey, get your arms by your ears, or something like that?'" she said.

Instead, the Ganims became grandparent figures to her even more than they had been at the gym. "As I got older, I was your typical teenager and didn't necessarily always think my mom was right, so I would always go over there." Ron would talk to her and she'd calm down a little bit. "He'd say 'You're fine,'" Alecia remembered. "That kind of stuff. It was nice."

When Alecia was a freshman in the 2013 state meet, the Bees' vault portion was so strong that people stopped to marvel. As a freshman, Alecia scored a 9.8 out of a possible 10 in the team portion of vault while two upperclassmen had scores above a 9.6. That made Brecksville's vault score more than 2 points higher than the next school. By her senior year, Alecia was a local celebrity. She scored the first perfect 10 in Ohio high school athletics history at a regular season meet.

If she competed for any other club gym, it's almost unthinkable that she would compete with the high school team. But being part of the high school team for her was a chance to bond with her teammates in a way that she would have never gotten as just a club gymnast. And she was happy to help contribute to the streak with meet-best scores that boosted their win chances every year. "It's just kind of cool to be a part of something that not only affected my life positively, but so many other people around Northeast Ohio," she said.

Alecia went on to compete at the University of Maryland—a poster featuring her and the team's schedule from her senior year hung on the wall at Gym World outside of Joan's office. And when away at college, Alecia said, she'd try to call Ron Ganim at least once a week to check in.

Her favorite memory of her old coach came when she was in college, when Ron told her that he was going to come cheer her on at her meet at the University of West Virginia. But then, at the last minute, he said he couldn't make it. She was sad but understood. She warmed up at the meet as usual, but in the middle of an event, she saw a familiar face: Ron had lied. He made it. Her own face crumpled out of excitement and joy in the middle of the meet. "I'm sobbing my eyes out because I'm so happy to see him," she said.

It wasn't really ever about just gymnastics, though. As her neighbors and her longtime coaches, the Ganims always just looked out for her, Alecia said. She had a tattoo on her wrist dedicated to Ron, an infinity symbol. When she graduated, she came back to coach at Gym World. "The Ganims were basically my family," she said.

. . .

Ron officially stepped down from his position with the high school team in 2012, after the team won its ninth straight title. His health declined to the point where traveling was difficult. "He didn't want to be depended on for being there and then have the kids get disappointed when he wasn't," Maria said. But he was still a frequent presence at the practices and meets. The gymnasts knew him—he had a knack for identifying when someone needed a pep talk or encouragement, many said. His retirement was announced at the end of the season and he was honored by his fellow coaches at the state meet. Ron Ganim was the kind of coach, they all said, who could be the fiercest competitor and then go grab a round of golf with all of the coaches he had inwardly (and outwardly at times) raged at. "Coach Ganim has impacted so many lives positively during his 34-year coaching career at BBHHS," the

Brecksville-Broadview Heights athletic director Dan Kalinsky told the *Cleveland Plain Dealer* at the time. "He instilled a fantastic work ethic amongst all of the athletes he worked with. He demanded a lot, but also had a unique ability to make it 'fun.' As I said at the sports awards, his athletes would run, tumble and vault through a wall for this man, which is the greatest compliment a coach can receive. He will be missed greatly by all of us."

. . .

It was a cold and snowy morning in Cleveland and Greg Ganim was fighting through the weather to get to Gym World to prepare the gym for a meet when his mom called, panicked.

His dad was unresponsive. An ambulance was on its way.

"It was a snowy day, so I went as fast as I could," he said. "Which meant twenty miles an hour all on the way home, which was really hard, you know? But yeah, he had a CPAP machine, and COPD and the oxygen level had been dropping recently. So if he didn't have that oxygen, the levels would go down quickly.

"My theory of what happened—and there's no video camera evidence here—my theory is that his mask fell off and or got moved in the middle of the night. And he woke up short of breath, sat up, and I think he just passed out without the mask on and no oxygen. We don't know how long he was there, but I think he, in my mind, just passed out, so he didn't even know what was going on.

"I'm gonna stick with that."

Ron never did wake up. He was seventy-two. After five decades of marriage, a successful business, and three children together, Joan was a widow.

At Ron's funeral, she remembered, it seemed like thousands of people came to pay respects.

"The line just went on forever," Joan said. "People came from everywhere. I mean, we had a person there from Chicago that came in for the wake, people from Columbus, Kentucky. Gymnastics people from all over the country and, over and over I just heard that he was just such a good guy and they could talk to him and he'd help. He helped them, and he was funny, but yet he could be really tough. It was just amazing, which I knew that, but it just went on and on and on and it was so many facets of his life."

Ron wasn't secretive but there were things that he couldn't tell his family about the kids he helped at work—but at his funeral, Greg felt like a new window was open into a world of kids his dad helped.

"These kids, they have children of their own now and they told us, 'I owe it all to him.'" he said.

Joan went back to Gym World as soon as she could following her husband's death. She just had to keep busy. It's what she had preached for years to her gymnasts—any issues stayed outside the gym. But it was hard. She still spoke to her late husband often. Of all of the things, that's the weirdest for her with him gone—it was not being able to talk to him at all hours of the day and night. "And being in the business, it's tough because there's days I need someone that I can just say what I want to say.

"But it's like with Ron, I thought of something at nine o'clock at night and I just go and we talk about it at nine o'clock at night. Or if it was ten o'clock at night, we would talk about something that was bothering either one of us that had to be fixed in the gym."

. . .

Three months after Ron's death, the Brecksville-Broadview Heights gymnastics team secured its fifteenth consecutive title.

It was a tough season, Maria, an assistant coach at the time, said.

Even if Ron wasn't at every meet and practice, the gymnasts had grown up with him. The school brought in grief counselors and the gymnasts wore bracelets to honor him.

When they won the state meet, they dedicated it to his memory.

"This win meant 10 times—a billion times more to me because it is the first year we have come to states and continued the streak, and still won with Mr. G being up in Heaven and watching down from above, just helping us every step of the way," senior Emily Huffman told Cleveland.com after the meet.

. . .

In 2019, Joan decided it was time for her to step down from the team as the head coach as well. She named Maria her successor, something that in a way seemed inevitable, but to Maria, it was shocking at the same time.

"When I took over for my mom, that first year I wanted to vomit because I said, 'Well ESPN hasn't covered us yet but now they might when I don't continue the legacy of what my parents have done, they will definitely cover that story,'" she said. "Or maybe we might get on *Ellen* because the streak is over."

It was also just a lot. In addition to gymnastics coaching, Maria was a successful and dedicated health teacher. She had won multiple awards for her work with middle school students' physical and mental health. She also had two children of her own.

Overnight, she went from being the person gymnasts saw as the fun assistant to the person whose name would—in her mind—be written forever in history books if the streak ended. It was her family's legacy, after all.

But she never thought twice about taking the role.

She spent most of that year nauseous. But she didn't need to worry. Her first year coaching the Bees won the state title, beating runner-up Brunswick by nearly 4 points.

In her second year, the Bees returned an experienced core and, though things were off because of the COVID-19 pandemic (something that shut down the country days after they won the title in 2020), they came home with another trophy. In 2022, the same experienced core was back and despite the anxiety following the bad balance beam performance, Maria was three for three in state titles as the head coach. She never relaxed, though. Every year she thought that this could be the year that they lose.

Her coteacher laughed at her at this point when she said that this could be it. "She goes, every time, Maria, every year I've been working with you, you say it's gonna be this year," Maria said.

Another colleague liked to tease her by asking if the bus broke down on the way to the state meet because, to him, that's the only way they could lose.

The truth was, though, that Joan never went far. She remained at most practices, meets, and team meetings. She was the person who helped the team perfect the balance beam routines and she's the grandmother figure who encouraged everyone just in the way that they needed it.

And, perhaps, just as importantly, Maria had Leah.

CHAPTER 4

Leah Miko

Leah's mom liked to tell the story of how her daughter surprised everyone from the start.

With a daughter and two sons, Rhonda Miko had her fourth child on the way. "Through the pregnancy, I get to my doctor and he does ultrasounds in his office sometimes, and he's doing an ultrasound and he's telling me, 'It's a healthy boy,'" she remembered.

She had not so secretly wanted a girl—a girl would balance out the family 50–50. Two boys, two girls, but a boy would be fine, as long as they were healthy.

On the day Leah was born, her mom drove to the hospital with a plan to deliver her healthy baby boy, the third in the family.

But that doctor, it turned out, had been wrong about one important detail.

"I had a C-section and lo and behold, it's Leah. And, you know, life has changed for the rest of my life," she said.

Leah was a mama's girl from the start, Rhonda said, and hated to be anywhere without her. The two were at the Brecksville Rec Center when Leah was about three and a half—Rhonda was taking a workout class with a friend and Leah was playing with some of the other kids close by.

Rhonda and her friend watched as Leah, out of nowhere, turned an impressive cartwheel on the rec center floor.

"Rhonda," her friend said, "you need to go to Gym World."

All of the Miko kids were involved in some sort of sports, but no one had tried gymnastics yet. Rhonda wasn't expecting a star—she just thought it would be a good way to get Leah a little bit less anxious when separated from her. "They had a really good reputation with [developing] girls with potential," she said of Gym World. "You know they're not shy about telling you it's probably not the right sport for you. And, you know, they're very good at allowing the girls that do have the ability to excel."

On Leah's first day, Rhonda thought she was probably drinking a juice box when she walked in. Leah loved juice boxes. "She was cute as a button," she said. She had probably watched the children's television show *Barney* at some point during the morning (it was another key thing that made her happy at the time). And her older sister, Erin, thought her hair was probably pulled back in a lower ponytail that her mom did, which was the style back in the late '90s.

And everyone agreed that upon first entering the gym, she cried. Leah told a newspaper in 2010 that it's because she was scared and didn't want to try something new. "I was used to tap and ballet and baseball. Gymnastics was something totally different," she said.

Despite her early reservations, Leah was quickly hooked. At Gym World, like most gymnastics places, there was a simple way to tell if you have skills. A gymnast either progresses into the next level or they don't. "Leah was in there to do something and make something of it," her mom said.

Early in her Gym World career, her dad, Bill Miko, found a balance beam at a garage sale (it was twelve inches off the ground, he clarified, not a full competition one, so she was fine if she fell off of it). It went into the Miko family basement, where Leah spent hours perfecting her beam routine, the part of the meet that was the most difficult throughout her career. When she wasn't doing that, she was flipping around in the backyard, her mom remembered. And anytime someone asked her to show off, she took it as a personal challenge. "She would not hesitate and just if someone wanted to see a flip, she would do a flip. I think she got as much enjoyment out of it as the person that was asking," Rhonda said.

They also had a trampoline in the backyard, but one day when they came back from a vacation visiting her grandparents in Florida, Leah was devastated to find a tree had fallen on it.

Erin, who is seven years older, always has a picture in her mind of Leah, tiny at the time, showing impressive dedication at an early age. "I distinctly remember this blue leotard that she used to wear that had sparkles on it that were like blue and black. And she'd come home and you know, not even in her sweats, sometimes she would just go in the car with her bag and get home and sit and eat dinner and do her homework and go to bed," Erin said.

Erin played basketball and volleyball and looked at her little sister, who had just completed a four-hour practice, and just shook her head. "She must be so tired," she would think.

But Leah, she said, was always determined in everything she did. She was a force. Erin remembered when Leah was in fifth grade and their brother Kyle accidentally got Leah's backpack all wet. "And they had notebook checks back then," Erin remembered. "Leah had come downstairs and maybe came home from practice and she goes into the laundry room to start working on her book report and grabs her book bag and everything is drenched and she starts crying.

"My dad's outside doing yard work. I'm not sure where my mom was. I just remember her crying and yelling and taking every single piece of paper and laying it around our entire basement so it could dry. And when I tell you how much these papers expanded to be put into a binder, I think that I laughed so hard—it is probably one of the top five funniest times of my entire life. I wasn't directly laughing at her, but the way that the papers expanded and her trying to put it back in the binder for her binder check was, I mean, it was hilarious.

"And obviously they ended up making up, but she was so upset that she was going to get in trouble with her teacher. She didn't wanna get a bad grade on the notebook check. So, you know, gosh darn it, those papers were gonna go back in that binder. If the binder was, you know, six feet tall, she was going to put them in there."

When Leah was thirteen, her parents split up. She was devastated and felt like she was the only one of all her friends going through something like that. And that's when she grew to depend even more on the Ganims and channeled a lot of her emotions into the gym. "I think she just found love and support from people outside of her dad and I, and I think that support was coupled with the sport that she was in. I mean, the Ganims are just natural parental figures, that's why their gym has succeeded as long and as powerfully as it has because they genuinely care about the girls that go there and they take them all under their wings," Rhonda said. "It gave her an outlet to get the frustrations out that she may have been experiencing."

When Leah joined the Bees in the fall of 2006, they were three years into the state title streak. She competed in bars for the team competition in her freshman year and her team easily won, beating the second-place team by six points. Back then, it was still a big deal to outsiders that the team won the state title—it wasn't as expected or routine as it became in later years.

Her brother, Shawn, was a senior at the time she was a freshman and she remembered his friends thinking it was notable she was on the championship-winning team. "All of my brother's friends said yeah, little Miko is on the gymnastics team. How cool is that?'"

It was just being on the team, though, that was the thing she valued the most. "Just the coaches, the atmosphere, the teammates, the sense of belonging," she said. "I just felt like that's exactly where I should be in that moment and I wouldn't change it for anything else."

By sophomore year, she was in three events in state meet and the meet was much closer—the team beat Magnificat by .35 of a point that year. In Leah's senior year, the team won easily—and Leah won the all-around on individual competition day. She had gone back and forth all season for the top score with her close friend Diana Moock. Bill said he realized she was going to win after she had a good performance on beam—the event that always tripped her up. She had already done well on vault. Bill leaned over to his family. "I think Leah may have done it," he said. With the state title, she was the best high school gymnast in the state of Ohio, gaining accolades in the *Cleveland Plain Dealer,* the local newspaper.

Years later, when asked about the win, Shawn treated with suspicion the question about what that was like as her big brother. "Did Leah tell you to ask that?" he wondered first.

It turned out that Shawn had been indebted to Leah since she won that state title. It was only the second time a Brecksville gymnast had done that in the past thirty-eight years. Shawn, then at Ohio State, had earlier made an offhand promise to his younger sister that if she won the state title, he would buy her a Range Rover.

Shawn did not expect his little sister to win a state title. Sure, he knew she was a good gymnast. But the best in the state? Thirteen years later, Leah was still waiting.

"It's never gonna happen," Rhonda said. "But I told him to get a Matchbox car and just give her a little one that she could sit on her desk at work at school."

That year also marked Brecksville's seventh team consecutive title.

. . .

Leah walked onto the gymnastics team at Bowling Green and as soon as she graduated with a degree in special education, returned to the Cleveland area. She started working as a teacher at the same school as her sister Erin, and outside of school hours found herself right back at home, this time as a coach at Gym World. She also became an assistant on her old high school team, joining Maria as one of the older sister-like fun figures behind Joan.

Leah was also one of a growing tree of assistant and head coaches in Ohio who came through Gym World. Going into the 2022–23 season, in addition to Leah, coaches at neighboring high schools Brunswick and Medina had ties to the Ganims and Gym World. But Leah's allegiance was almost unmatched. And as she told it, the timing and the circumstances just worked out. There are dozens of gymnasts who would have coached with them, she said. She's just the one with a job schedule that allowed it and had happened to move back to Cleveland.

But it was likely more than that.

It started with the Ganims being the people she looked to during another tough moment in life: the end of her gymnastics career. For Leah, it had been her whole life. And just like that, she was just another former gymnast. "And the first two people I turned to were Mr. and Mrs. G. and they helped me to see what that transition looks like. I've only known gymnastics my whole life, and those two really guided me through," she said. "And then they said, you know, the best way to keep gymnastics in your life is coaching. And they suckered me in a little black hole.

"And I haven't left since. I started coaching at 21 when I was done with gymnastics in college. I think that was the reason why I started coaching club, coaching preschool classes, which was the worst time of my life."

She paused for a moment.

"I will never coach preschool ever again."

. . .

Going into the 2022–23 season, Leah was the longest tenured current assistant coach outside of the Ganim family on the team and Maria's most trusted adviser. While Maria was the head coach, Leah was the first voice often heard at Brecksville gymnastics practices and competitions.

As a coach, she had to grow and change her coaching methods and focus in real time. She started as an assistant when she was twenty-two and had constantly thought about what she needed to do better. She was closer to the gymnasts' age than Maria and Joan and had more recent experience actually doing the skills that the coaches are asking the gymnasts to do. She also, Maria said, just had more energy. And no one was more enthusiastic after a good routine than Leah. She's the quickest to be next to her gymnast with a bear hug and a loud cheer. Parents of opposing teams often grumbled in the stands that she was over the top. She's also the one who was quick to make them do conditioning ("Leah loves suicide sprints," one gymnast who practiced with the team said of the running drill that Leah favored. Conditioning, in general, seemed to be her favorite thing.)

Leah poured everything into her gymnasts.

And she had that combination of coaching magic that made her team trust her. "She's my coach, but she's also kind of a friend," said Rachel Kelly. "It doesn't seem like she's just my coach. I feel like I can talk to her about whatever, it doesn't have to be gymnastics related and I can goof off and it just is normal. I feel like I can be a gymnast and a person at the same time around her."

Leah was still learning, though, and even with eight years of experience coaching, spent a lot of time thinking between seasons about what she's going to do differently. Going into the 2022–23 season, she thought she would be better about making the gymnasts fight through something when it wasn't going well. Her dad Bill was a baseball coach and said she spoke to him about the issues she has coaching, which, he said, often were related to the mental side of gymnastics.

She'd known most of the gymnasts since she coached them in club when they were younger at Gym World. Because she had watched them grow up, her desire for them to succeed often matched the responsibility she felt to the Ganims, her second family, to keep the state win streak going.

To get through their anxiety, Leah and Maria developed some routines of their own.

When the team is competing on the balance beam, the two stand on opposite sides. "If a gymnast falls, we blame ourselves," Leah explained.

Clearly, according to their logic, they were standing on the wrong sides. So, if something went wrong, they silently rotated. In the 2022 state meet, they rotated five times and it didn't help. But it didn't stop them from carrying on the same tradition into the 2023 season. They had to sit in the exact same seats on the bus. It was all part of being a Brecksville gymnastics coach—or even a gymnast. Maria had even more. In the vault event, she was always at the back of the runway. She never remembered a time when she did otherwise. Joan based her superstitions on the location of her purse, which she needed with her during the meet at all times.

"She has her little worries too," Maria said. "We all have our little worries that we gotta make sure, because if we don't say it out loud, it's not gonna happen."

Maria also had to make sure she walked through the threshold into the gym at the state meet a certain way, a tradition dating back years. She would only walk through with her left foot first, leaving her sometimes shuffling in a weird manner to make sure she wasn't cursing the team with improper walking through the door. She wasn't sure if the gymnasts even knew she was doing it.

"And it's very weird," she said. "And then if there's during state meet, if we were successful on the first event, I have to do whatever I did before, like if it was—that I walked in whatever door and came out, or if I went to the bathroom in between the rotation or I went into the coach's room and got water, I have to do that every time.

"It's superstitious. I know I have no control. My dad used to tell me all the time, 'You don't have control over what happens, you know, and the outcome of that, it's not gonna make a difference.'"

Maria, then and now, strongly disagreed with him. "Yes," she told him. "It is."

The Brecksville gymnasts may not have known how many superstitions the coaches had, but part of being a Brecksville gymnast included following a long list of traditions and superstitions of their own. From hairstyles to premeet meals, being a part of the Brecksville gymnastics team was carrying on not only a tradition of a state title streak but all of the traditions and rituals that the team strongly believed got them there.

And it's not just up to them.

Bees parents, as they quickly learned in their first preseason meeting, when their daughters were freshmen, had a long to-do list.

After all, like Maria, Leah, and the rest of the coaching staff, their daughters were the stewards of the streak. And that could be (at least temporarily) life-altering for everybody.

CHAPTER 5

Ella and Delaney

In early November, the weather was starting to turn cold, but not quite yet the bone-chilling cold that often defined Cleveland winters. The gymnasts crowded into the classroom-style loft room above the main floor at Gym World to talk about the season. There were eighteen of them—eight freshmen (Carol Samuel, Rachel Kirin, Kyla Haverdill, Bailey Miller, Emily Gromek, Veronica Yakushchenko, Sara Kwiatkowski, and Brooke Smerdel); four sophomores (Ava Audino, GG, Avery, and Rachel); four juniors (Jeanne Winzen, Lea Haverdill, Abby Henning, and Tessa Long); and two seniors (Ella and Delaney).

Maria stood up front while Joan sat behind her in a chair in the corner. Ella and Delaney sat nervously in the middle of the group. Ella had long brown curly hair and Delaney's was shorter and dirty blonde. Both were wearing hoodies.

Since they had joined the team as freshmen, Ella and Delaney were aware that this day would come. As the sole members of the class of 2023, it was their time to be team captains—the voice of the team and the leaders whom their younger teammates would come to for advice.

The youngest of three children, Ella started gymnastics at Gym World when she was in preschool and, like the rest of the Bees, had just stayed with it. It was pretty simple—she liked it, was good at it, and just kept going. "I used to walk around my house on my hands and just see how long I could do it for and walk around the island in my kitchen as many times as possible or even do a handstand on top of the island because I could press up to a handstand," she said. She remembered the first time she could do a back handspring, something she was so excited about she shared it with her teacher. "I remember writing it in my journal in first grade, my first back handspring," she said.

Her mom, Kim Shaheen, remembered when she brought Ella to try out for the PETS (petite elite training system) when she was five. "She was all for it when I talked to her about it, in the weeks leading up to it," Kim said. "And we drive there that day and Ella was so shy, we didn't even get in the building and she says 'I don't want to do this.'"

Kim knew her daughter had been so excited about it and would regret not giving it a chance so she "picked her up and I walked in with her screaming," she said.

One of the longtime Gym World coaches, Caroline Nun, came out to talk to Ella. They came to an agreement that Kim would come into the tryout with her. Kim and Ella sat on the side as the group started doing the first test, which was to see if the gymnasts could do a pull-up or hold their chin over the bar for a length of time.

Kim turned to her daughter and tried a bit of reverse psychology. "Ella, that looks really hard," she said. "I'm not sure you can do that."

Five-year-old Ella, determined, stood up and looked at her mom. "Yes," she said. "I can."

She walked over to the bar and did the exercise.

Kim left the room.

Ella never looked back.

More than a decade later of dedicating much of her nonschool time to gymnastics, her skills that she's the most proud of are a little more advanced than the ones she wrote about in her first grade notebook. "I was really excited when I got a double off of bars (a highly skilled dismount) because I was just working to get that for so long. It's not really consistent, so I don't think I'll be competing it again, but I was really excited when I got that."

Ella knew she was going to join the high school team since she was in middle school and saw her friends from her club team join it. "And then I figured out that we had the winning streak and I really wanted to be a part of a winning team," she said.

Ella, a level 9 gymnast, competed in the state meet lineup for the past three years and was expected to contribute to all four events in her senior year. She competed in the individual state meet events for three years, her second during the year that was most affected by COVID-19. It was a weird one that's always stuck with her. Usually during the state meet, the team stayed to cheer everyone on—it's one of the things that makes high school gymnastics fun. Even on the individual day, everything is loud.

But the world was on pause during her sophomore year.

That year, though, was still filled with moments that she treasured. The small group of Brecksville-Broadview Heights state meet individual day competitors rode home on a team bus—a comparatively quiet one compared to the raucous one that follows state meet normally—and the gymnasts turned to Leah. As a group, they had an impressive meet. Ella finished second in the meet on the bars, followed by Lindsay at third, and senior Kaitlyn Dembie in fourth. Ella had finished eleventh in the all-around. Kaitlyn finished third, Erin fourth, and Lindsay in seventh. They were thrilled. It had been a weird year and they had still managed to perform well. And sitting on the bus, they were hungry. They campaigned Leah successfully to have the bus stop at Raising Cane's, a fast-food restaurant that specialized in chicken fingers.

"I don't know why but it was exciting because we really wanted to go through the drive-thru on a bus," Ella remembered. Because they didn't eat much before competitions, it was the first food of the day and something that never would have happened if the full squad had been on the bus. "It was so good," Ella said.

It was always the random moments like that, the ones where she became closer with her teammates over seemingly benign happenings that made her love gymnastics the most. Ella loved gymnastics because she liked the challenge of learning new skills and impressing herself when she was able to master them. But the best part was just being able to hang out in the gym for three hours a day with her friends.

Going into her senior season, Ella also had another chicken-related tradition that she had helped start to carry on. It started the night before the 2022 state meet when then-senior Lindsay Kern had ordered a chicken dish at a local Italian restaurant. It tasted off.

"I can't even eat this," she said. Then she asked Ella to take a bite to make sure the whole thing was bad.

"I took a bite," Ella said. "And I was like, yep, it's bad. And then everyone said, 'Wait, I need to try it to see how bad it is.'"

Each teammate took a bite of the offending chicken. ("It had mold on it and it was so gross," Rachel Kelly claimed. Others said it was undercooked.)

"At the end of the dinner," Ella explained, "We said 'We can't forget this because it was so just so funny at the moment.'"

So the chicken was stored in a plastic bag and went home first with Erin. She transferred it to a brown paper bag and wrote in clear letters two words: "Lucky Chicken."

The lucky chicken traveled to the state meet that year. And then, at the end of the meet, Erin passed it onto Ella for safekeeping.

The chicken then traveled back to Brecksville and to Ella's house.

She told her parents that they were not to touch the lucky chicken, now in their freezer, and after three years of Brecksville gymnastics traditions, they knew better than to question her.

Going into the first team meeting of the 2022–23 season, Lindsay and Erin were away at college. The chicken remained untouched in the Shaheen freezer.

It would remain there until the 2023 state meet.

. . .

Delaney, a level 8 gymnast, had a similar start with gymnastics. She started at Gym World as a little kid and just kept going. When she was in middle school, like Ella, she realized she'd likely be on the high school team. It was just, she said, what everyone who was at that level of gymnastics at Gym World does. She competed for the first time in the state meet as a last-minute swap in her junior year. When one of her teammates couldn't compete at the last minute in the floor routine, Delaney, without having even warmed up, didn't hesitate. "I can go," she told the coaches. Going into her senior year, she was focused on making it in the state lineup, not as an alternate. She spent the offseason working with her club coaches to make what's called upgrades to her routines—adding new skills and sharpening old ones to make her routines worth more points and therefore more likely to land her on the state meet lineup.

Like Ella, she wanted to be a team captain because she felt like it was her responsibility and she wanted to pass on all the lessons, help, and encouragement she'd gotten as an underclassman. Plus, they were the lone seniors. It was their responsibility to step up to lead the team. But neither of them really liked speaking in front of people, so they sat nervously as Maria started her speech.

. . .

Maria looked over at the group of gymnasts who would be entrusted to carry the team's legacy in the 2022–23 season.

She and Joan had known most of them since they were preschoolers or at least grade schoolers at Gym World, and Leah had known them since she returned to Gym World as a coach. The gymnasts knew about the high school team somewhat in the background throughout their lives, with most of them understanding they would be part of it by middle school, when many of them had Maria as a health teacher.

And even though they were older than those small kids running around Gym World in their early years, they were . . . young, the youngest group the Bees had had in a long, long time. And the largest group too. Back in the 1990s and early 2000s, it was common to have thirty girls on the team. Some gymnasts would join the high school team having never trained at Gym World just as a way to get involved in an activity. But that hadn't happened in years. This large and skewing young group was going to be a big change from last year's senior-heavy starting state lineup.

Maria started with the basics and had everyone go around and introduce themselves. It was a bit unnecessary—between Gym World and school, there wasn't really anyone who didn't know anyone else.

"All right," Maria said, putting on her reading glasses. "We've got a lot of freshmen this year. So let's go over all the stuff we need to do. You should each have your physical form. Did we run out? Yay. Or did everyone get one? We have plenty. Okay. All right. So everybody, I checked the final forms this morning. I think we're good."

She noticed three girls who didn't have their paperwork up to date. They all promised to get on it immediately.

"Perfect. All right," Maria continued. The next order of business was GPAs. She warned the gymnasts to make sure that they not only were keeping up their grades but had a sufficient amount of credit hours to qualify academically. "That's the one where we've actually had a gymnast in the second quarter have an issue. The grades come up at the end of second quarter and all of a sudden, they're ineligible. So if you're not sure, ask your counselor.

"Attendance. Obviously, attendance is mandatory. It's part of earning your letter. If you are going to be absent, you need to not only text me and Leah, which we've talked about, we'll talk about the texting, making sure that Leah and I are both on it or another adult. But if you're a club gymnast, you still have to call Gym World. If it's our Saturday practice, it's just me. But if it's a club practice that you're getting high school credit for, you need to tell me and you need to tell the front desk."

The girls nodded. Maria continued.

"You are expected to be at every practice from start to finish. Even if you are injured, you are still expected to be there. If you're going to physical therapy or something like that, that's just something you need to talk to us about. Three unexcused absences will be a dismissal from the team. An unexcused absence includes continued tardiness or early leaving. It will result also in loss of points. Possible removal, like if you get an unexcused absence, could be a possible removal from the event or a competition.

"That's to be fair to your teammates who do show up and are on time. Excused absences will include illness, doctor's appointment, student council, PT, vacations. I've told your families if you're going on a vacation, and some of them have already told me when you're gonna miss, but make sure we know as soon as possible. I already can't remember. I know, Abby, you're missing. I know, Sarah, you are, but I already can't remember the dates in my head. I know when I look at the email. So when it's closer to that time, just say, remember, I'm not gonna be at this meet or I'm missing, you know, for whatever," she said.

Next item of business: practice attire.

"You gotta wear a leo and compression shorts. No T-shirts, sweatshirts, boxers. I think we all know that. Grips for bars, obviously hair tied up, one stud earring allowed. Do not plan to get your ears pierced during this time because you cannot wear any jewelry in an Ohio high school competition. So you're not allowed to have any, even if USAG allows it, high school does not. And if they can see the piercing through leotards or whatever, if it's on your belly button, you gotta tape it up because they've seen them before. If it's in your nose, take it out. You're not allowed to wear any of that. All right, so for competitions, it depends on the meet."

She took a breath. The next part she really needed them to hear: As long as they were going for the state title, this was not a team with equal meet time.

"How many gymnasts we can put in each event. It depends on what meet we're at in the season. Everybody will have the opportunity to compete multiple times, I hope.

"But when it comes to postseason, it's top six average scores. That's gonna be the bottom line. The only way we're gonna try to get someone else in is a senior if we get that opportunity. But we are not promising it. I only have two seniors here. They both had the opportunity to be in a high school state meet before.

"It's if we wanna win—do we wanna win? That's a decision that when you talk to the captains without me and Leah around and Mrs. G. If you decide it's not about continuing the streak of winning state meet, that's totally fine. I've been a part of state titles before. All right? What we have to decide is if we want to put our best team out there or get everybody a chance to compete. This is a varsity sport, but we don't cut.

"But you have to understand, too, then that there's that risk. This is the most we've had on a team in years, so it'll be very unique. We used to have thirty on a team, though, and some of those girls never stepped foot into a varsity composition even when we had three squads.

"You're part of a winning team. And that's the best part of it. Keep those positive attitudes, respect your coaches and teammates at all times. Have a good work ethic."

She knew the team would never take her up on the alternative of winning the state title. They couldn't possibly decide before the season they weren't going to continue a state title tradition that had started before they were born. Even if it was up to them, it really wasn't. Part of being part of the state title winning team was carrying on a tradition for women who were decades older than they were. It wouldn't just be their team they were letting down if they opted out—it would be everyone who had contributed in the past to it too. And, of course, the legacy of Ron and Joan Ganim.

But Maria still had to say it. She needed to be able to point back to it to the gymnasts who had come after the season or years after their careers, livid that they hadn't been put in the state lineup. After a slight pause, she transitioned back to the matter-of-fact rules. Medicine procedures. School attendance (if you're absent you can't practice). Phone use: limit it ("if you need to use it, just bring it outside of the locker room and just tell us 'Hey I need to text my mom' if you need to. Don't try to sneak it.") "Especially during states," she said. "We just need to be careful, especially when we don't know the results or the scores. We can't be distracted. Leah and I and Mrs. G have the direct line up to the stands at what's happening, all right? But I want you to just focus on competing and being there for your teammates and not worrying about that."

She went into uniforms and team attire. The gymnasts perked up especially for this. Sweatshirts, Jeanne said, should be Nike. They were nicer than the current ones.

Maria took the suggestion into account. "The only thing we have to keep in mind is the freshmen have a lot of expenses coming up extra," she said.

After a few more items (including Maria's new favorite advice to her son that she wanted the team to keep in mind: "Don't do stupid"), it was time for the captains' speeches. Maria looked up. She kind of knew what to expect but wanted to give an unexpected candidate the last-minute chance to jump in.

"If you wanted to run for captain, this is your opportunity to tell your teammates why you'd like to be captain and what your role is, and then I'll pass out some pencils so that we can vote."

Ella was up first. She held an index card in her hand with some points she wanted to make.

"Hi, I'm Ella and I'm a senior," she started. "I've been on the team for four years, since my freshman year. And I think I would be a really good captain because I've been in the sport for forever, so I know what a lot of people go through. And also being a club gymnast, I also can be your voice to the coaches for our practices that they're not at. For just high school people, I'll also be there every Saturday. I also will try to make it more fun, but even with the fun, I want us to win, so I won't make it too fun."

The team laughed.

"I hope everyone agrees with that."

The team applauded. Then, it was Delaney's turn.

"Hi, I'm Delaney. I've also been on the team for all four years and the team means a lot to me. I hope I can lead this team, help us become closer with each other. I'm on the Athlete's Council for club gymnastics, so it's helped me become a better leader, which I hope to use as captain for this team also."

The team applauded again.

Maria looked around. "Anybody else wanna run for captain? You're able to, you don't have to be a senior. Well then, all in favor of these two being our captain, put hands up."

Everyone raised a hand.

"Oh, look at that—100 percent. I can't remember the last time that happened. Congratulations," Maria said. "Congratulations, captains, and good luck. You've already been great. Thank you. I've already reached out to them to do certain things being that they were seniors not knowing if they were gonna run or not. I appreciate it already. Any questions that anybody has and don't be afraid to ask. It's like in class, someone else might be thinking the same thing, so just ask away."

While waiting for additional questions, Maria glanced at the schedule.

The first high school meet was five weeks away. It was also the week as a club meet that honored her late father and that she was pretty sure a number of club gymnasts were going to compete in it. The Brecksville-Broadview Heights team was made up of primarily club gymnasts, as they're called, or gymnasts who compete for Gymnastics World. (If a gymnast zoned to Brecksville-Broadview Heights competed for another club gym, they were still more than welcome on the high school team; it's just rare that that happened.) In order to be eligible for regional and national club meets, the club gymnasts needed to compete in a certain number of meets for events as determined by their club coaches in December or January to qualify. So, many of the gymnasts were scheduled to compete the next week at the Ron Ganim Invitational, a meet at Gym World.

But the day after that meet was the high school season opener, where Maria also needed gymnasts to fill the rosters. Maria asked for a show of hands. "If you're a non-club girl, raise your hand," she said.

She counted four: Abby, Kyla, Tessa, and Brooke. The rest were so-called "club girls."

Carol, Sara, and Veronica all practiced together at Gym World Twinsburg in the Excel program, meant for gymnasts who competed at level 6 or 7.

Veronica hadn't been sure about competing for the Brecksville team at first. As an eighth grader, she wasn't competing at as high a level as some of the other gymnasts on the Bees had and was worried she'd embarrass herself. "I was afraid I wasn't going to be good enough to uphold this very big streak that was going on," she remembered. She had mentioned something about it in health class, which she had with Maria. "Coach Schneider pulled me to the side. I had a class with her in eighth grade and she was telling me all about how you don't have to be the best and you don't have to do perfect routines all the time. It's just for fun and if you put the work in you can win stuff. It just really made me want to do it."

Sara said despite Veronica's doubts, they had all talked about joining the team forever. "All the time," she said. "We'd say, 'Hey, are you excited? Have you signed up? Have you talked to Schneidy?' We all have always known we were Brecksville gymnasts; it was really exciting being able to all go into it together."

She was a little nervous in the first meeting, but mostly just excited to be part of something with such a legacy. "It's just such a fun and exciting thing to join," Sara said.

GG, Jeanne, Rachel, Ella, Delaney, Lea, Emily, Bailey, and Avery practiced at Gym World Broadview Heights, competing at levels 8–10.

The group who competed just for the high school team practiced a few times during the week with Leah and Maria while the rest of the team was at club practice.

All of them at one point had gone to Gym World as club gymnasts but decided at some point to just do the high school team. Brooke left the club team when she was twelve, and was excited to be back in the sport for her freshman year. "I missed the girls who I always practiced with because I was on a team with them for pretty much my whole childhood," she said. "I just missed that. I missed the friendships that I would make and I missed the work ethic." It would be fun, she thought, to get back on a team. But a few weeks before the season started, she hurt her ankle in gym class—she was focused, at the start, on just being the best teammate.

Tessa competed at Gym World until she got to high school and then decided she just wanted to focus on the high school team. Now a junior, she remembered as a middle schooler looking with admiration at the older gymnasts who competed for the high school.

"I didn't know them personally, but we all knew who they were because of the streak and we all thought it was really cool," she said. She joined the team because she wanted to be part of that and treasured the friendships that came with it. "We all go through the same thing at practice and stuff, we always have something to talk about and it's just fun to do [things] with your friends."

When it came to the first meet, though, the four gymnasts who didn't compete club wouldn't be enough to fill the lineup for a regular season meet. Maria needed six gymnasts in each event. Maria sighed. "Every club girl is going to be ready if we want to put you in on Monday the 12th?"

Most of them nodded. She gave another warning that they were expected to compete for the team, even if it was watered-down routines.

Then she tried to get the conversation back on track with more about the schedule. She marked off that one gymnast was going to be gone the week of Thanksgiving. Finally, the meeting was over. "All right, well congratulations to Ella and Delaney," she said and the gymnasts started to file out.

Maria and Joan watched them head back down the stairs and past the gym floor.

The drive to the twentieth consecutive state title had officially begun. And this, really, they swore, could be one of the toughest years yet.

. . .

A few weeks earlier, the parents of the gymnasts had crammed into the same room. Like the gymnasts, most of them knew Maria, Joan, and Leah well. With few exceptions, their daughters had competed at Gym World since they were small children. They knew Maria from her role as a teacher as well. But for the parents of the freshmen, this year was different. This was the first year that their children were responsible for carrying on the state win streak.

Maria started off with a similar speech that she had given the gymnasts. This was a varsity sport. A spot at the state meet—unless the gymnasts decided they wanted to do something differently this year—was not guaranteed. She needed the parents to know that to reinforce this if any of the gymnasts didn't hear her the first time. And she needed them to know what they were getting into as well.

The parents were also responsible for funding, arranging, and in many other ways assisting all of the traditions—some sacred for their good luck value, others just for fun—that had been part of the team for decades.

An early tradition in the season was an easy—but important-point of awareness. The gymnasts wore their team leo to school (along with pants) one day during the season. In the past, some freshmen had thought that the older gymnasts had played a trick on them. But no, Maria said, it really is a tradition.

Maria continued ticking off all the idiosyncrasies and small points she could remember.

The gymnasts liked to wear red crocs for meets. "We arrive at the bus fifteen minutes before the bus is scheduled to leave," Maria said. "We will leave you. It has happened before. We'll leave you—well, Leah will leave you. She's the one who will leave."

Maria tried to think of more traditions to be aware of. There was a journal, called the Fish, that was passed around each season. That tradition, too, was older than the girls—it was started even before the streak. The gymnasts take turns throughout the season writing in the Fish a letter of encouragement to the next teammate.

Kim Shaheen looked around at the nervous group to relay some of her experiences. As one of two seniors' parents, she was familiar with this. She knew that they were getting ready to be in line for all the volunteer opportunities, which were year-round—not just during the season—and that all parents really needed to pitch in. And the team dinners.

She remembered the feeling as a freshman parent. The other parents listed all the events and responsibilities and little things to keep track of. "How," Kim remembered thinking, "am I going to remember all of this?"

Going into her fourth year as a Bees parent, she felt better, but as a senior parent, she also had more responsibility. And she had to be the calm authority for the influx of freshmen parents scribbling down notes.

Before each meet of the season, a parent hosted the entire team for dinner (there was a sign-up sheet for that). The dinners had started as spaghetti dinners but had evolved a bit in the past twenty years. It could be at a restaurant or at their house. In addition to food, the host also had to supply the hair ribbon for the meet—the team all had to wear the same and this was the easiest way to coordinate. "Do the girls tell you what color or are the parents picking?" one freshman mom asked.

"I would pick out a few and get my daughter's blessing," Kim said.

One of the fathers interjected. "If I'm hosting the dinner, I'm picking the ribbons. When I did this for the O-Line during football season, I didn't have to do this with ribbons," he grumbled.

The group laughed.

Maria clicked through the costs that the parents might expect: the registration fee for the sport, the potential for sweats, and, if they needed them, new uniforms. To help make the team's ends meet, the parents were expected to help with fundraising, which meant working at the concession stands at other sporting events (there was another sign-up sheet for that). There were more ideas tossed around—a baked goods sale at school was a popular one. Also, with so many new parents, they needed to fill the official position of treasurer to handle all the team's funds that would be raised from multiple fundraising opportunities that were being coordinated.

The freshmen parents began to look overwhelmed. To get to this point, they had all poured thousands of dollars and a large portion of their daughters' lives to the Ganims and Gym World. But they could already tell: This was going to be at a different level.

Maria remembered one more thing: the songs. The girls, she said, would sing the altered alma mater on the bus. Maria and Joan tried to remember the words. They got it together confidently by the third line. "Vault, bars, beams and floor, scoring on our opponents, points for us to score. Honor Brecksville, honor Brecksville, on our way to states. So squeeze your butts girls."

The parents laughed again.

There was also a cheer that the parents had to learn. Nearly two decades earlier, in the early 2000s, gymnast Kristy Ryan's dad Bruce came up with a cheer that had stayed with the Bees. The parents, in a quiet moment in the meet (you certainly couldn't do it while someone was competing), would chant as loudly as they could "BE" and then the team would echo back "ES." (Throughout the season this would prove harder than it seemed when first explained.)

Kim continued with a few more things the parents should know. "I had the honor of hosting last year and I'll do it this year. After the state meet, it's tradition that they go out toilet papering," Kim said.

"Not mine," Joan interjected.

"It's a sleepover, they don't have to sleep over if they don't want to, but it will be early in the morning if they need a ride home," Kim said. "And then the senior girls usually write a letter to each girl to read on their way to the state meet so they can read them on the bus. And then prior to senior dinner, all of the girls write letters to the seniors and those get collected and put in the gift that they get at the end of the year. One of the things that's on the volunteer list as well is we always decorate the bus for the state meets so anyone that wants to contribute to that is greatly appreciated. It's not just going to be the person that signs up, everyone can contribute, but that person can coordinate. We just can't cover the windows and things like that, but we hang streamers and signs and their pictures and we give gifts. It's a big thing for them so we try to make it special."

Even at the parents' meeting, weeks before the season started, it was a nonstarter that the result of that season would be anything but at least going to the state meet.

Maria looked around.

"Freshmen parents, this seems very overwhelming and this is a year, too, where there's a lot of extra money. This is the year where you're investing for the next four years, for their uniforms and warm-ups and everything and all of the other things that were mentioned. I get it, that's why we're trying to offset those costs if we do them . . . if you have any quick easy ideas, if you're having family financial issues, please talk to us. We don't want them to not be on the team because of that; we can figure something out always."

The room was quiet for a minute.

After a few more minutes of discussing fundraising ideas, Maria had one more reminder about the dates of the season's start. It was a month away.

She asked if there were any more questions. Of course, she knew, there were. But the parents were a bit too dazed to ask. For the freshmen parents, their lives were about to change. Their girls were now on the best high school gymnastics team in state history.

And for the parents who had been here before, they all had a picture of the season going forward in the back of their minds, hoping that their girls wouldn't be on the team that broke the streak. And, at the same time, hoping they would get to play a big role in keeping it alive.

CHAPTER 6

Season Opener

Lea Haverdill, a junior with brown hair and green eyes, knew the Ganim family, especially Maria, since she was a baby. Her dad Todd was Maria's teaching partner at the middle school. As a small kid, Lea was so shy that "if I knew she was coming, I'd go grab M&Ms to give to her so she would talk to me," Maria said.

Todd later switched to the high school, where he once taught Leah Miko in class. "I've always been super close with them," Lea said of the Brecksville-Broadview Heights coaches.

There was never really a question that she and her two younger sisters would be on the high school team roster. "I just always knew that that's the path I was taking," Lea said. And she was good at it. She competed in the state meet lineup on the uneven bars as a freshman, helping the team to its eighteenth consecutive title. She made it to be a level 8 gymnast in club gymnastics. She spent thirty hours a week at the gym. Her little sister, Kyla, followed her in the same path, two years behind.

But then in Lea's sophomore year, she was hurt badly. She tore her ATFL ligament in her ankle, right at the start of the high school season. A doctor told her she could try taping it up and competing and have surgery in the offseason. So she tried taping it and doing everything she could to limit the pain. Her mom Melissa was a physical therapist so she did as much work outside the gym as she could. "But I hit a wall," Lea remembered. She decided to end her season and have lateral ankle reconstruction surgery to repair it and was sidelined for months. She remained a cheerleader of the team and was even passed down the boom speaker from the upperclassmen to make her the official team hype music leader going into her junior year. And that's when, taking that forced break, she began to realize something. "My body felt so much better, having that time to rest and not being full go every day," she said. "We never really had a break. And having that time, being forced to take that break because of surgery really opened my eyes on how much better my body felt and which made it way easier to do gymnastics."

Lea was cleared to start practicing again in October after nearly ten months off. For most gymnasts, the high school offseason was spent doing upgrades in hope of doing better the next year. For Lea, it was spent relearning how to do the sport. "I was just focused on getting my everything back, reteaching myself everything I knew how to do before. It was all about consistency. I didn't upgrade any of my routines from last year to this year. They're just all the same, but those last two months I was just working on consistency and getting back to it."

But something was different. She didn't want to feel that same constant pain anymore. So Lea made a decision.

She decided to stop competing in club gymnastics and just focus on the high school team. It meant instead of practicing six days a week, she would be down to two or three days a week, three hours a day maximum. Maria understood. "I didn't look at it as her being a quitter or anything like that to leave the club team. She just was done physically and mentally with it. So that wasn't going to do her any good by continuing it," she said.

Lea wanted to compete in one more club meet, the Ron Ganim Invitational. "I just wanted to have a good ending to my club gymnastics career," she said.

She did well. She came in second all-around for level 8, finished in second in beam and bars and third in vault and floor. And then, just like that, she was done. Her entire focus would be on the high school team and the new possibilities for the vast amount of free time that she had just opened up. She thought she might try the track team in her senior year.

It felt weird, though.

"That was all I knew my whole life," she said. She hadn't remembered taking more than a week off since she started gymnastics. "It's all I did my entire life."

Two days later, the Bees started their season.

. . .

The high school season opened for the Bees in the gym at Brecksville-Broadview Heights School. They converted it into four quadrants for each event, and parents, teachers, siblings, and friends dotted the bleachers. Around the gym, the Bees championship banners covered the walls. For the Bees, the first meet of the season, one where Rachel (illness) and GG (club team) were missing from the lineup, was mostly about just getting out the jitters.

Or trying to.

"Having eight freshmen compete for the first time in front of their classmates and peers is a lot different than a club experience if they were in club before," Maria said. "Anytime in front of their peers is stressful."

For Ella, her first meet as a senior captain, the preparation began in the morning. She ate a bigger breakfast than she normally did to prepare for a late dinner. And she made sure to hydrate throughout the day.

"The nerves don't really hit me until right before," she said. "It's just a normal school day."

"After school," Delaney added, "that's when I get nervous."

Then, once the team started setting up for the meet, the nerves came in waves. "It goes away," Ella said. "And then it comes right before I compete and then it goes away again." Ella competed in the club meet only a few days before, earning first in that meet on the uneven bars, so she felt confident going into her uneven bars performance at the first meet. Her routine was supposed to be press handstand, toe handstand ("Which is you put both of your feet and shoot up to a handstand"), jump to the high bar, cast handstand, giant half, giant half layout. But halfway through the routine, she felt herself just trying to fight to not fall off. It wasn't her best performance. She was frustrated. She walked off quickly after her performance for a moment to move past it.

But Ella knew it was early in the season. And she had competed in three state meets in her three years in high school. She wasn't too worried about her spot in the state lineup, at least not yet.

If anything, she and Delaney were trying their best to be strong leaders in their first official meet as team captains. "I feel like there's more pressure to make sure everyone else is ready before they go," Delaney said.

Before the meet, the advice the seniors had given everyone was simple. "We know what we're doing," they said. "We know we can hit our routines. Just do your best."

For the freshmen, it was an eye-opening experience into what a different world high school gymnastics would be with the pressure to perform to get on the roster for state meet and with your friends and family watching. Bailey's head was spinning. She went into her bar routine and quickly fell off after the nerves and noise overcame her. "I just couldn't hit anything," she said.

The team had an oversized chain necklace with a glittery yellow Bee that was ceremoniously put around the neck of each gymnast after she hit a routine. It was adopted from college teams they had seen do a similar thing. It was just one of the traditions that made the Bees a little louder, flashier, and enthusiastic at times than their competition and promoted team unity. If the gymnasts stuck a routine—usually they had to stick the dismount, no steps—then they got the bee.

The standards were lowered for the first meet, though. "Today we said 'If you make your routine, you get the bee,'" Maria said. The gymnasts wore the bee until the next gymnast hit her routine and it was passed off.

Delaney had spent the offseason working on upgrades to her routines, fighting for a spot in the state lineup that was guaranteed instead of as an alternate. It was her senior year. She knew that especially when it came to her floor routine, she could do it. "Because I can just have fun and not worry too much."

And coming out for her first meet as a senior, she caught her coaches' and her team's eye. She finished second on floor, but after the meet, as the announcements blared through the speaker, Ella said it was "the best routine I had ever seen her do."

Brecksville gymnasts were together for so many hours a week that they had each other's routines memorized (the routines had also been passed down from former gymnasts, so many of them had seen the same ones for years). In Ella's floor routine, there's a point where she clapped twice. The entire team, which lined the mat during the competition, clapped along with her in perfect sync. Watching her cocaptain, Ella knew from having seen Delaney's routine so many times previously that Delaney had upgraded her first pass in the high school offseason to be more difficult. And it paid off.

"It was really clean and her second pass was really clean this year too," she said.

Maria noticed too. It was one of her highlights of the meet. "She showed quite an improvement," she said.

Lea, in her first meet as only a high school gymnast, came in first on uneven bars.

Maria was also thrilled that Ava Audino hit her first tsuk vault, which means she did a quarter turn onto the horse and then a backflip off of it. Ava, a junior, competed in club at Gym World until tenth grade, when she decided she wanted to focus on just the high school team. She had been working on a tsuk for months. In practice, she would park at a vault table with mats stacked up and completed a series of drills designed to help her land it. "Some days I would land a bunch and then some days I would land none," she said. "It just took me a while to be able to get the hang of, and then it took a lot of fails that I wouldn't land."

When she landed it, her teammates rushed over to celebrate. "It just felt really good because it showed my training and practice paid off," she said. It was a good start to the season, she thought.

Bailey also shook off the nerves by vault—it's one of her best events. She hoped that she could earn a spot in the lineup for the state meet and was thrilled when she placed second in it. She wasn't the only freshman who made a good early first impression: Emily came in third on uneven bars.

Delaney and Ella took their captain's roles seriously and Delaney especially tried to set an example and helped the freshmen understand their roles in building team culture and ensured that they followed an important rule: Never just sit. That meant that the freshmen, when not competing, were quick to move mats, change equipment settings, or go find whatever someone might be looking for. By the end of the first meet, the underclassmen were in a constant flurry of activity, moving mats on cue with impressive speed throughout events without being asked. The team also had to set up and break down the meets in the gym with only the help of their parents and sympathetic siblings and occasionally significant others. Maria often reminded the gymnasts' families that taking down after meets counted as volunteer hours for anyone who may have needed them for school requirements. But that call for help was rarely heeded. It's one of the things she and Joan hated the most about competing at the high school.

Another part of team culture that Delaney and Ella and all of the Bees took very seriously was team bonding activities. One of the early traditions of the season was to build gingerbread houses together in December at one of the gymnasts' houses. Before the second meet of the year, they gathered at Ella's house. "Instead of hosting a team dinner for Saturday's meet, Alicia and I are going to provide pizza and other snacks after the meet. All girls are welcome over to my house to make gingerbread houses," Ella's mom Kim wrote in the group chat. "There will be five teams of girls to compete against each other on who can make the cutest gingerbread house. This will be after the meet and after showers :)."

"Also," she added, "we are still in need of some parents to sign up for team dinners."

At Ella's house after the meet, the girls wrote their names on small pieces of paper and then put them in a bowl. The team leaders picked the names at random and divided up to test their skills. Some of the teams struggled, and their gingerbread houses fell under the weight of bad construction or too many extras. But Ella's team had a strategy. They knew that the judges, Ella's parents, tended to favor more colorful gingerbread houses. Ella confidently led the group to make a colorful house with neat rows of decorations and took home first place.

The randomness of the teams was important, Avery said. "You were with people that you might not have talked to as much as others. And building gingerbread houses takes a lot of teamwork and it just helped everyone grow closer, I think, because they all had to work together to make what they wanted happen." Delaney noted that her team's gingerbread house stayed standing up, a true accomplishment for the event, even if they did not win.

. . .

Rachel could barely get herself out of bed before the first meet.

Maria may have needed her to fill out the lineup, but she had caught some sort of bug that sidelined her—she missed school with a sore throat, fever, and general wooziness.

In club gymnastics, she was a level 8. Short with blonde hair and brown eyes, she's bubbly and often was one of the loudest voices on the team. Headed into her sophomore year, she was expected to be an all-around contributor and one of the best gymnasts on the team. Leah and Maria had her penciled in to have scores that counted for four events—a huge accomplishment for an underclassman. She knew they were counting on her—and Leah often reminded her. "Make sure you're working hard," she told her. "We need you."

She also, despite being just a sophomore, was one of the team leaders—quick to cheer on her team (which, as a varsity cheerleader, came naturally to her) and was often the leader of fun at team bonding events, on bus rides, and in practice.

One of her earliest contributions of the season was, along with Lea, being responsible for the 2023 team hashtag: "justrock" which came from the Lil Uzi Vert song that became a TikTok sensation.

The two approached Leah first with the idea that this was their team song. But Leah shot them down. "No, I don't like this song," she said. "Why would this be our song?"

Rachel and Lea were undeterred. "No," they told her. "It has to be our song, we just wanna rock."

Leah held firm. They were frustrated. But at the next full team practice, Leah surprised them.

"Guys," the assistant coach announced. "Our new hashtag is #just-rock."

Rachel and Lea looked at her, confused and excited.

"Yeah, I was listening to it," she told them. "I think it's a pretty good song for us."

Lea and Rachel were thrilled.

The first time Rachel and her mom Jessica saw Brecksville was when they lived in Erie, Pennsylvania. Rachel was a young gymnast—a level 4 at the time—and in elementary school and in town for the Rock and Roll Classic. "We were super early," Jessica remembered.

They drove around, went to get something to eat at a nearby fast-food place, and then drove through the neighborhoods near Gym World. "Wow, this is really nice," Jessica told Rachel, who was sitting in the back seat of the car at the time. "You know, if I ever lived in Cleveland, this would be the neighborhood that we live in."

The family's next home was in Ohio—in Columbus. Jessica worked in hospitality management and got a job with a hotel there. Rachel started training at Buckeye Gymnastics, the club gym where Olympian Gabby Douglas also once trained. She used to see her during some conditioning portions of practice, which even back as a young kid, she thought was cool. But then, by a twist of fate related to Jessica's work, they found themselves moving to Cleveland.

Jessica asked Rachel's gymnastics coaches in Columbus for advice on where they should go for Rachel's gymnastics. Her coaches said Gym World, next to the neighborhood that Jessica had already unknowingly picked out a few years earlier.

There were houses for rent right across the street from the gym, Jessica remembered. After Rachel's tryout went well, they rented one and a few months later, they bought their house in Brecksville, which was close to the high school and Gym World.

Rachel, now a sophomore, was in fourth grade at the time and quickly started building friendships with gymnasts who would later be her high school teammates. Sitting at her kitchen table, wearing sweats after practice, she ticked off the timeline of how she met her teammates. She met GG, who lived around the corner from her, when she was trying out because she was in the group that Rachel was put into to try out at Gym World. She met Rachel Kirin, who was a year younger, at Gym World shortly after. Ava rode the same bus to school. A few years later, when she was a level 8, she met Lea. In middle school, she had Maria as a health teacher and that's when it really hit her, she said, when she heard her talk about the high school team and the streak. "And that's when I think I realized, I thought oh my God, that'll be me in two years," she said.

Jessica often thought that if they had stayed in Columbus, Rachel wouldn't have really ever heard of Gym World. Instead, now she was competing to be part of their history—and had an important role on the team.

"I just knew that if we lived in this area and we went to Gym World, that she'd be on the high school team. It's a given," Jessica said. "But I had no idea about the streak that they were on. Last year being that freshman mom, it was, oh my gosh. It's a big deal. Their story is incredible, the whole history of this family, this gym, and it's just incredible. It's really awesome to be a part of it. I just hope it happens for them. If it doesn't, it'll be a quiet bus ride home."

She laughed.

"But I think it will be just fine. But like I said, we had no idea."

Even though she had started at the gym later than the other gymnasts, Rachel had the same sense of duty to keep the streak alive. She remembered Mr. Ganim, always wearing a white T-shirt and shorts and wheeling his wheelchair around the lobby of Gym World. She was close to Joan, who was one of her club coaches. "She makes everyone happy and positive," she said.

And to her, carrying on the streak wasn't a question. "It was made before I was born and obviously, we want to continue it," she said. "I feel like it's also a thing to continue for Mr. G, he coached the team. He coached Mrs. Schneider when she was on it. I just feel like it's a thing that winning is carrying on for him."

In the offseason heading into her sophomore season, Rachel planned on spending time perfecting her routines as they were. Instead, she realized that she could add bigger skills to her routines—skills that were worth more points and could make an impact on the team's standing. The coaches knew that going into her sophomore year, she had the potential to have a major impact on the team. It also put a lot more pressure on Rachel.

Rachel's biggest challenge often, though, like many gymnasts, was herself. She was a brilliant gymnast, her coaches would tell her.

They just needed her to believe that.

But she was far from the only one who often doubted herself.

Luckily, at Gym World, the coaches spent a lot of time on the psychological side of gymnastics. In fact, it's one of the things they proudly thought made them stand out.

It all went back to Ron and Joan, who saw an opportunity to help and motivate gymnasts in creative and healthy ways.

And, in some cases, it was just a matter of practicality.

. . .

At some point in the 1990s (no one was quite sure when, but Maria knew she was away at college), Ron started a rotation during the club gymnastics practices where gymnasts talked about their feelings, learned methods to better focus and reduce stress during competition, healthy eating, and more. The actual content varied through the years and it was taken up by Maria after her father's passing as a weekly class for gymnasts. It's called Psychobabble.

"I would love to say it was simply my dad's forward thinking and him being able to understand the importance of it," AJ Ganim said. "But I think there was a bit of function." Once it started, it proved popular with the gymnasts and their families—and it worked for the purpose of freeing up valuable gym space. Ron was tickled by the success.

"We did it in one of the old rooms that was upstairs that was probably used as a closet kind of thing," former Brecksville-Broadview Heights and Gym World gymnast Christina Lenny said. "This was before they built the second gym in Broadview Heights. I remember us sitting on these therapy tables and mats and stuff that were in there and we would have it in there."

And they would just talk, she said. Or write things down in notebooks. "I thought it was great because everybody thinks or talks about how physical gymnastics is, which it is, it is super physical. You need to be in shape and conditioned and trained properly. But it is also mental," she said. "And that was the one thing—we would talk about so many things in there, whether it was goal setting or something else, there were so many different topics."

"We talked about families, we talked about friends, we talked about being teenagers and everything," Kristy Ryan remembered. "All of the temptations and stuff and how to be a good person and how to handle stressors. I can manage time very well and I really truly think it's from gymnastics. We were able to handle working out five days a week, school, friends, family, and you just learn how to manage your time."

Sometimes, Alecia Farina remembered, the guest speakers took them through exercises that seemed completely far-fetched. One that she remembered had the gymnasts put a magnet at the end of a fishing line and just keep holding it. "Basically, it was you could make the magnet kind of rotate in whatever way your brain was looking at it. So it was just one of those things that was, you know, no matter what it is, some way or another, your brain is everything that you need to get through no matter what you're doing in life," she said.

Even without *Psychobabble* as an official term and class, Greg said that as Ron's son, he experienced talking about feelings, focus, and more daily. "I could tell you it was just always, always Psychobabble in everything we did. He's just a teacher at heart; that's what he does."

Since Maria was also a health teacher, she took over Psychobabble after her dad passed away. Leading that rotation meant taking on a bigger role in Gym World than she had previously. It was also a lot: She had two sons, a full-time job as a health teacher, was an assistant coach for the high school, and taking over Psychobabble meant she was now in charge of one rotation a week for a large number of gymnasts at Gym World. And, she wasn't sure she could step in for her dad. "I didn't know if I could do it as well as he did, that was my big thing," she said.

But just as with when she took over coaching, there was no way she was going to let her family down and say no.

Going into the 2022 season, it had been five years since Maria took over. She thought about changing the name—there's something about it, she thought, that sounded too flippant or politically incorrect. But she hadn't put her finger on what it would be that would actually mean she should change it yet. Under Maria's watch, Psychobabble included a lot of goal setting. She's always tried to keep up with the times of what is on the minds of teenagers.

"It's changed from when my dad focused on nutrition, what they're going to eat, you know, their goals, their fears. It's evolved. Because there's so much more that kids have going on in their lives than they did twenty years ago when it all was starting."

She started to tick off all the pressures that teenagers are facing: social media, to start. She had no idea what her dad would think of TikTok, Instagram, and Snapchat and how much they affected gymnasts' ability to concentrate in the gym.

"Their minds are all over the place. They're more worried about what they said to their friend in the middle of classes and thinking that that friend's gonna be mad or they didn't like a post. I mean, not all of them, but a lot of them."

Plus, they're more worried, she thought, than ever about getting into college and test scores and expectations put on them academically. "I see it because I'm teaching and I don't know if people realize how kids have it now with school and the pressure that we're putting on them. And I just think about that elementary kids barely even have recess. Middle school. Forget it. You know, if we give them twenty minutes past lunchtime, it's too much and they can get in trouble, but they need that downtime, that socialization piece," she said. "But our society is go, go, go, go, go. We don't stop. And their brains don't ever stop. And social media, it doesn't allow their brains to stop. And so that's the big difference."

She purchased the Calm app, a meditation, sleep, and mindfulness app and did meditation and other exercises on it with the gymnasts. She had slideshows about healthy eating and fear. They talked about goal setting. They did vision boards.

Some of the gymnasts, she knew, hated it. "There's some kids that can't be put into those settings. I always try to offer if this makes you uncomfortable, you just need to let me know and we can do something else." The gymnasts also sometimes journaled or just talked about what was going on in their lives. But most of them, especially the Brecksville high school team, leaned heavily on the skills and coping mechanisms they learned. Some of them even worked with sports psychologists for extra help.

. . .

The second meet of the season, held at Gym World Twinsburg (about twenty minutes east of Gym World Broadview Heights) was a low-stakes friendly meet—the Bees were competing against Hudson, Walsh, Padua, and Revere—two teams that practice with Brecksville (Padua and Revere) and two that they're relatively friendly with. Before the meet, Rachel warned her coaches, she did not feel ready to go 100 percent. "My body," she told them, "is still weak."

Leah told her to take it easy on her routines. After all, it was early. "If it was the postseason," Rachel laughed, "she would have told me to suck it up."

She knew going into the meet that she still felt weak and wasn't expecting to do that well.

Rachel watered down her routines and competed an easier vault than she was expected to in the postseason. But she was pleasantly surprised—Rachel ended up winning the all-around and taking second on floor exercise—an event that above all other events requires gymnasts to look like they're having fun and confident and not flu-ridden. Ella took third in the all-around and tied with Emily for first on vault. Jeanne earned first in uneven bars and Bailey, in her second meet as a Bee, took third on vault. Lea finished first on balance beam and behind Jeanne for second on uneven bars. Delaney came in third in the meet on balance beam. GG didn't compete yet because of her club schedule.

As a team, Brecksville scored a 142.35. There were mitigating factors, of course: GG wasn't competing. Rachel was sick. The lineup that competed likely wasn't the lineup that would compete in the state meet. But the score was low. To the team, this was a low team score that they wouldn't ever think was an acceptable outcome in a meet that counted.

By comparison to the rest of the state, if they had competed that score in the 2022 meet, they would have finished in the top six. Leah and Maria were as encouraging as they could be as they turned the attention toward the next meet. Leah wrote in a caption on Instagram after the meet: "Go BEES! #justrock #theperfect20"

. . .

Despite the positive Instagram captions, the low meet scores were in everyone's head. As the team huddled in Gym World for a practice on a cold Saturday, anxiety was written in the faces and the mistakes the gymnasts were making across the floor.

The coaches wondered if the gymnasts had just thought too much that they would just walk in and win another state title and were taken aback that the scores weren't as high as they used to be. Some gymnasts thought it was just because everyone was worried about securing their spot—with so much turnover from last year, there was a real chance to take a spot to be in the lineup in state. Rachel thought the team was just in a funk because the full lineup wasn't in. Ava thought it was because they had been weary of the competition after seeing some early high scores. Jeanne thought it was because they lacked some confidence. Avery, now a sophomore, agreed—she thought a large sense of insecurity came from knowing that, at least to start, the team potentially wasn't as strong as it had been in previous years when it had a core of gymnasts who had been in the state lineup, which, on a positive side, left open opportunities for everyone to step up and get their spot. "Obviously it's everyone's goal that they want to be in the lineup," she said.

Avery, a level 8 club gymnast, went to preschool next to Gym World, and her parents had signed her up for gymnastics class. The family already knew the Ganims—her older sisters cheered at AJ Ganim's gym, Cheer World (later renamed World Elite). At first, Avery remembered wanting to do cheerleading with her sisters instead. But soon, she missed gymnastics. "I asked my mom, 'Can I go back?' And then she let me and then I've just been doing it ever since."

Jocelyn remembered being impressed by Avery's skills even from a young age. They would drop her off at practice and then pick her up a few hours later. "We really never saw anything. We wouldn't watch her until she had a gymnastics meet. And that's when you see what they're doing and the skills that she has progressed to and is competing at whatever level it was."

The meets, she remembered, were amazing each time—it filled in a story of only partial bits that came from Avery after practice. "I mean, she would come home and explain it to us, but we never really knew what the names of certain skills are," Jocelyn remembered. No one in her family had ever competed in gymnastics—and certainly not to the level of dedication Avery showed at a young age.

Going into sophomore year, Avery had a simple goal: to just keep improving her skills to make sure she had a spot in the state lineup. Despite slipping off the balance beam in the state meet as a freshman, she was strong in that event and hoped to make it a second time as a sophomore. In a team that had a lot of anxiety about the beam, Avery was a rarity: She loved it. "It's just me and the beam; there's not really anything else to it and sometimes I'll listen to the floor music that's playing and just do my dances to it and I just do my skills and try not to overthink it."

The year before, in her state debut in her freshman year, Avery didn't know she was going to be on for beam until the very last minute—and she wasn't sure anything would ever match the pressure she felt at that moment. "They didn't tell us the lineup until right when we were walking out because they were deciding on our warmup and at that time, I was the alternate so I wasn't expecting to be in the lineup. It was really surprising."

The coaches, as practice, would not tell the gymnasts the lineup for any meet, states, or regular season—even the night before. They wanted, Leah said, for everyone to be ready to contribute in every event at any time.

But the last-minute beam changes, in retrospect, were all part of the mess that had Leah and Maria in tears at the end of the 2022 meet. This year, the coaches were focused on beam being different—being a strength. And Avery, they knew, could be a big part of that. She finished third in beam in the first meet of the season. She still had time, she knew. The regular season was all about adding new skills to routines and eliminating mistakes.

Leah thought there were positive signs across the team. It was only the second meet and she had seen some of the freshmen step up more than she had expected, this early in the season. One of them, Emily Gromek, tall with brown hair and a concentrated expression that instantly sparked a reminder from Joan to smile each time she competed, finished first on the vault in the Bees' win.

. . .

Emily was coming back from a club meet in Kentucky and passing through Columbus as an eighth grader when she decided, on a whim, to go check out the high school state meet. She was unsure whether she was going to join the high school team until then—she was a level 8 gymnast with a possibility to compete at the next level if she kept her focus on gymnastics. Club gymnastics traditionally would have been the focus if she wanted to make sure she put herself in the best spot to make a college team. But sitting in the bleachers at the state meet, Emily's mom Jennifer watched as she took it all in. The cheering. The camaraderie. The energy. And then GG competed for Brecksville as a freshman on the vault.

At club meets, where Emily and the other gymnasts competed until high school, the atmosphere was much more subdued. It's not that people weren't friendly—they were—they'd competed against and trained with many of the other gymnasts for years. The parents traveled to the same meets for years too and generally gravitated toward the other families they were used to seeing. But it wasn't the high school team. The high school team's energy was one where everyone was deeply invested in every gymnast's performance in each event. High school gymnastics was a team, and even the best gymnast can't carry a team to a title by themselves.

So Emily, then in eighth grade, sat and watched intently. The vault was already Emily's favorite event. Jennifer watched as her daughter's eyes followed GG's vault. And that's, Jennifer thought, when the decision was made. Emily wanted to do what GG did on the vault in front of the cheering crowd and teammates. On the car ride home, Jennifer remembered, Emily talked about how cool the atmosphere was and just how loud and energetic it all was. It was unlike anything she'd ever seen in her gymnastics career—one that began when her daycare center, like Avery's, happened to be next to a gymnastics gym.

"They had what they call this little rainbow program," Jennifer remembered. "In the summer, we would sign her up for it and then the daycare walked any of the kids over there that got to do these rainbow gyms. And she's fearless. She always has been. So she loved the trampoline, anything that keeps her active. She also did ballet and tap dance at the same time." By the time Emily was seven years old, a gymnastics coach saw Emily's promise and told Jennifer that she really needed to sign her up for the competitive team.

"But the practices that summer were at such a weird time and I didn't know that we could get her to and from. And by the fall, the team coach came up to me and said we really need to get her on the team. We made the switch. She was at level 3. She was about four months of training behind [current teammates] Kyla and Bailey."

Emily broke in with what she remembers most from this story. She had to be held back a level. Well, not exactly held back, her mom clarified. She repeated that year because she was struggling on her front hip circles. But gymnastics was drifting quickly toward an all-consuming activity. And so was dance.

"They had her in contemporary and ballet and all this other stuff. She had to make a choice." Jennifer laid out the problem as pretty simple math to Emily, then eight. Dance, she said, was three or four nights a week, as was gymnastics. "I didn't know how to squeeze it all in," Jennifer said. She'd pick Emily up from dance and Emily's brother, Noah, would be sitting in the back of the car doing his homework. It didn't make sense for them to go home because they had to go to gymnastics.

"I just told her, I said, you get to choose," Jennifer said. "And I thought for sure she was gonna choose dance for whatever reason. You know, she was so elegant and so cute with her hair up in the bun."

Emily didn't hesitate. She turned to her mom and said, "I've made my choice. I want to do gymnastics."

"It was the right thing for her to do because it's a big commitment and if she wasn't engaged with it, it'd be hard to get her out of bed for a Saturday practice, whether it was ballet or gymnastics," Jennifer said.

Emily took it very seriously. "She's extremely hard on herself and she's her own motor inside just pushing herself," Jennifer said. "She thinks she's going to let other people down and her dad and I just constantly remind her that as long as you're giving it 110 percent, you can have a bad day and you just shake it off."

Since that day when she chose gymnastics, Emily has tried other sports too—softball, soccer, basketball, a volleyball camp. "But gymnastics was just the one thing that she latched onto and stuck with," her mom said.

So five years after she chose Gymnastics World over dance class, Emily sat in the car ride home from the high school state meet in Columbus and made another big gymnastics commitment.

She decided to become a Bee.

Maria and Leah knew Emily from Gym World, so when they heard she was in, they were thrilled. In addition to being an impressive gymnast, Emily also had a maturity beyond her years—she was hard to faze, even in the early days of high school gymnastics.

Though, once on the high school team, she realized, it's definitely different. Even practices were high stakes. "Every single turn matters and every routine is important," she said. "I have never been in that environment before. People have never been cheering this much. It's never been this loud. So especially at practice, I'm making sure I do pressure sets—routines where they're purposely trying to distract me to get ready for a state meet," she said.

Emily was surprised to find herself on the roster for four events in her second meet—a sign that the coaches were considering her to be a major contributor, possibly to the postseason, though it was still early. "I didn't know I would be contributing in that many events," she said. "But I'm happy to."

. . .

In Cleveland, the months from November to late March were consistently gray and drizzly with frequent bouts of lake-effect snowstorms that didn't show up on the radar or weather reports beforehand. Longtime residents knew to plan a vacation for January to somewhere where it's just a little warmer to break up the monotony of gray. Winter break for school went from the week of Christmas through the first week of the new year. And while Leah and Maria knew that some families went on vacation—and didn't exactly discourage it—the gymnastics season started to feel short after the new year. So they didn't exactly encourage it either.

"Here's what's happening over break," Maria wrote to the parents in mid-December. "Saturday 12/17 bus leaves at 3:15 from the GW parking lot. Meet 5:30—I expect us to be home by 8 P.M. or earlier. Monday-Wednesday normal practice schedule for all. 12/11—GW [Gymnastics World] club team parties). 12/22—4:30–7:00 PRACTICE (club girls can attend if want but not mandatory). 12/26- 10–12, 12/27—MEET 10 A.M.—bus TBD once I get the schedule, 12/29—3–6, 12/30—3–6. CLUB girls—I am confirming with Jared (one of the club coaches) what practices you will attend, but most will be with us. AS ALWAYS subject to change but I am fairly confident in the schedule right now."

For the coaches and parents, juggling schedules required a high degree of organization. In high school preseason, a club gymnast's schedule would look something like:

> Monday (club practice) 4–8 P.M.
> Tuesday—no practice

Wednesday (club practice) 4–8 P.M.
Thursday (club practice) 4–8 P.M.
Friday—no practice
Saturday—no practice
Sunday (high school practice) 9–11 A.M.

Once the season started, it could look more like:

Monday (club practice) 4–8 P.M.
Tuesday (club practice) 4–8 P.M.
Wednesday (fundraising activity) After school
Thursday (club practice) 4–8 P.M.
Friday (team dinner and meet setup)
Saturday (high school meet)—Bus at 8 A.M.
Sunday (high school practice)—9–11 A.M.

Club girls usually practiced with their club coach multiple times a week and only came to high school practice a single day during the week and the weekends. Their club coaches worked with them on skills needed for club and high school competitions and were quick to text Maria or Leah if a gymnast added a skill that could be useful to incorporate into high school.

When asked how the Brecksville team was so good, Maria would often quickly point to their club coaches. For the handful of gymnasts who are on just the high school team, they'd attend high school practices during the week and one on weekends.

At Christmas, Maria wrote to the parents: "May your day be filled with beautiful memories spent with your loved ones." Then, a reminder. "Practice tomorrow 10–12. Thank you for allowing us to coach your daughters! Maria, Leah and Mrs G."

The third meet of the year was at Crossroads Elite Gymnastics, a private gym in Strongsville, a suburb further on the west side of Cleveland. The night before the meet, Bailey hosted a team dinner at Chipotle (it was a relatively subdued one because of the holidays). The bus was scheduled to leave at 8 A.M. two days after Christmas. But when they got there, there was a slight problem.

Snow. Not just any kind of snow. Lake-effect snow—the kind of snow that didn't show up on the radar and piled up quickly.

A message appeared from Leah's phone at 7:49 A.M. the morning of the meet in the parents' group chat. "Hi this is Maria. Bus frozen gate and now plowed. Some girls leah and [I] can drive to meet but if you have an issue with this please advise asap. Going to reach out to parents of drivers but of course my phone isn't working."

Abby's mother was the first to respond. "Abby can take people in her car you have our permission." A few minutes later a message from Leah's phone popped back in. "bus is now coming!" Two parents responded with smiley face and thumbs-up emojis. Finally, Maria's phone was back in order with some news about rules and regulations from the school. "Apparently these kids can't drive themselves. We are still waiting for a bus."

Emily's mom Jennifer chimed in. "Do we need to caravan the kids there? I can drive. I understand the bus is still not there."

But that wasn't allowed either. "We are still waiting. I was told bus was on its way half hour ago," Maria typed. "Still waiting." She was fuming. The joke her coteacher always made that the only way they would lose the state title streak was if the bus broke down on the way echoed loudly in her head.

The third meet of the year—this one against Strongsville and Padua—wasn't that big of a deal. Regular season meets, especially early in the season, never were. But she worried if it was an omen. Bailey's dad asked if the meet was going to be on time or delayed. "Plans to be on time!" Maria replied. "We had wiggle room for warm-up because a team canceled."

Finally, the bus arrived. They made it to the meet and won. Rachel took second on vault, bars, and all-around; Emily took third on vault; Jeanne took third on bars; and Delaney finished second on floor exercise. "Bees with the dub 🐝 #justrock #beesonthree #STB #23in23 #busdriver," the Instagram caption read.

Lea Haverdill added in the comments, "rocked."

As the days ticked to end 2022, the Bees spent the cold and cloudy week at practice, finding solace in the warm gym as the rest of Brecksville and Broadview Heights huddled inside. A video posted to the team's Instagram account started with Emily practicing on the beam and ended with Ella perfecting her bar routine, "sweating the details here for the bees #bees #23in23 #theperfect20 #stb #justrock #lfg"

Maria laid out the schedule for the month: "Sunday practice 10–1 GW Broadview. 2. Sunday team dinner 6:30 P.M. at Kwiatkowski home 3. Lakewood meet bus: 5:00 P.M. 4. 1/14 9–12 at GW Broadview 5. 7:30 team dinner at HS and then we will ALL set up for 8:30 senior night/ beauty and the Beast 6. 1/19 Senior night—more details forthcoming. 1/22 10–1 GW Broadview 6. 1/26 home meet- we will need to set up RIGHT after school for this one—need lots of help! Meet 6:30 P.M. 7. Friday Jan 27th—girls being invited to Monsters' Hockey game and will be recognized. More details coming soon. 8. 1/29 10–1 GW Broadview 9. 2/4 8–10 GW Broadview," she wrote. "I hope I have it all correct . . . I know I will make a mistake. Bear with me. It's a lot to juggle."

Abby's mom was the first to reply with some much-needed help. "Let me know ASAP if you need Abby to set up high school volunteers through key club the students are interested to help but she needs to get it on the schedule thanks!"

Maria was thrilled. "Yes please!" she replied, rattling off some dates.

Emily's mom did a double take at the late senior night setup. "Dinner at 8 P.M.??? Why so late?" she asked. Set up not until 9?"

"We can't get in to set up til 8:30 P.M. in the gym. The team dinner will be before that at the HS so then we can start earlier by getting everything out of the room and close to the doors of the gym."

It was one of the harsh realities of life for the Bees. They may have been the nineteenth consecutive state champions. But they still were just a team looking to share gym time with the other varsity sports.

A few days after Maria laid out the hectic month ahead, the Bees gymnasts showed off what they were up to at practice in an Instagram post "3 new vaults added to the line up today," Leah wrote in the caption. "LFG."

But even as she was writing confidently on Instagram posts, Leah and Maria knew they had a problem. Rachel, one of the team's best gymnasts who was being counted on as an all-around competitor at the state meet, couldn't do her competition-level vault. She hadn't been able to do it since the season started. At first, they thought it was because of her flu. But weeks later, she hadn't gotten it back.

She had been through this before. Over the past two summers, she had worked hard to improve her skills, especially the ones that her team needed. And in the past two seasons, she had been in a good spot going into the season and then had mental blocks that stopped her from being able to compete or perform what she had practiced.

When she could do it, it was one of her best events. Leah, Maria, and her team were counting on her to get a high score in it in the postseason—when she competed for her club team, after her freshman high school season, she averaged over a 9.4 in it in competition.

But mentally, her head was telling her that she couldn't do the vault. Gymnastics, after all, is a sport where competitors have to overcome the natural warnings in their brain often and convince themselves that circling around a bar high in the air, walking on narrow beams, or doing a backward handspring is a good idea. And Rachel had no idea how to convince her mind that it was okay to go backward onto the vault or in a floor routine. Maria had seen it before too and was at a loss. Rachel was far from the first gymnast to have a mental block—they all had them. A lot of gymnastics required gymnasts tricking their brain into doing something complicated and potentially dangerous. But usually that fear went away in a week or so. "It's out of my control at that point," Maria said. "They're teenage kids. I'm not here to win at all costs. It's just not me. Their health is more important and even if it's their mental health, that's more important to me." So she just waited to see if Rachel would be able to clear it up. It was all she could do.

CHAPTER 7

The Math Problem

"What I always tell the girls is beam and bars are what allow you to win the state title," Leah said. "If we're not good on beam and bars, then there's no hope."

And at the start of a teamwide practice the first Sunday in January, there was not a lot of hope.

Alumni Lindsay Kern and Erin Delahunty sat on the floor chatting with Leah and watching a portion of the team practice on the uneven bars. They were back from college for winter break and grimaced as they watched mistake after mistake after mistake on the bars. They watched as Jeanne went up for her routine on uneven bars and crashed so hard on her back that a coach had to tell her to take a break. She walked away from the mat, grimacing. Sugar Ray blasted through the gym—one of the artists that's part of the late 1990s, early 2000s playlist Leah insisted on playing at practices. Earlier that day, she had had her usual exchange with Abby, a talented musician, about a song from the early 2000s she played that the high school junior had liked but didn't recognize. It was the rap artist Eminem.

"Who is this?" Leah would ask.

"Tupac," Abby would reply. It was always her answer if she didn't know the artist.

Leah then pretended to be beside herself.

It cracked them up every time.

On the balance beam, more gymnasts wobbled and hopped off prematurely as Joan gently pointed out small mistakes that could be costly. Everyone looked out of sorts.

Erin and Lindsay had tracked the team's progress throughout the season from their respective colleges and were as alarmed as the team had expressed after the second meet about their low scores. Neither of them had gone on to compete at the college level so they hadn't competed in nearly nine months, but at that moment as mistakes flew around the gym, Leah and Maria looked like they would take them back on the high school team if somehow that was allowed.

Maria watched from the center of the gym where she scrolled through her phone, looking at the scores from other teams that she had seen over the weekend.

"We are starting to freak out," Maria said. "Team in Columbus went over 146 today and Brunswick over 145. Leah and I are off our rockers today."

It didn't necessarily mean anything. Scoring at regular season meets could vary—a judge who scored meets in Columbus, for example, could be more lenient than the ones who worked the Brecksville-Broadview Heights meets. But it was definitely unnerving.

Leah and Maria scouted teams by watching social media posts and live streams and whatever other video she could find on the internet. "You kind of do your own way to scout as best you can because you can't see all the teams," she said.

She also texted with other coaches. It's a small community and there were schools nearby that Leah and Maria always had their eyes on and knew from their years in the sport. Many of them had trained at Gym World. Medina, the team that had threatened them last year, was on their radar. Brunswick, another Cleveland-area school. Magnificat, their longtime rival. But it was really Olentangy Berlin High School in Columbus—a school she wouldn't get to see before the state meet—that had her worried. They tied for sixth in the 2022 meet, five points behind Brecksville, but this year they added Tayten Swain, a freshman sensation who had been scoring higher in the all-around than the individual all-around state champion in the 2022 state meet.

"They have some really good gymnasts," Maria said. And thanks in large part to Tayten and some other talented gymnasts, their scores she had been tracking were high—higher than Brecksville. And the worst part was she wouldn't see them in person before the state meet, so she had to judge their skills through videos posted to social media channels and through what she heard from coaches she knew who had competed against them at a recent invitational.

In the weeks leading up to the practice, the Brecksville team won all three of their meets easily. But a win didn't really mean anything for their state title goal. Instead, Maria and Leah were focused only on the scores the gymnasts earned in their routines—and who had started to look like a consistent competitor they could rely on in the state lineup.

At this point, they were really only competing against themselves. Because they decided that winning a state title was the goal at the beginning of the season, how they were performing in the regular season meets—outside of building confidence and helping the coaches determine the state lineup—didn't matter. They thought that a 147 team score would be a goal to aim for this year with their current lineup.

It hadn't always been that way.

For nearly a decade, between 2004 and 2014, the Bees didn't lose a single meet in the regular or postseason. They compiled an almost secondary streak, winning 777 meets in a row. But one day, in 2014, because they needed to make a lineup change to make sure they were ready for the state meet, they simply lost in a regular season meet, ending the streak. They were defeated by Magnificat, 133.15–126.8. Magnificat coach Joe Gura told the *Cleveland Plain Dealer* at the time that his team was "very excited, and they should be. We understand that they did not have all of their athletes, but to beat them is something our team should be very proud of. I thought our team performed very well tonight, and we have to keep it up and keep improving throughout the rest of the season."

In the only comment printed from the Brecksville coaches in the article, Ron Ganim, then technically retired, pointed out to the reporter that Brecksville had rested its top three gymnasts.

When asked about it years later, everyone associated with the Brecksville program shrugged and brushed aside that moment that it ended. It just hadn't mattered enough to them because by resting the top three gymnasts, they were able to achieve the real goal of the season: Brecksville went on to win the state title with a 144.625 team score. Magnificat came in sixth in the state meet that year.

Each year to win the state title, the Brecksville coaches were faced with essentially a math problem. A complicated, ever-changing, completely unpredictable math problem, but a math problem nonetheless. There were four events—bar, beam, vault, and floor and six gymnasts from Brecksville competed in each. Of those six gymnasts, the top four scores are counted. When the gymnasts competed in club, they competed the toughest routine possible. But in high school it's different—they had to compete to win as a team. So, the coaches designed routines that could add up to enough to be the top score at the meet. They based their calculations on what they thought their team and each gymnast could most reliably do and also what they thought would be enough to beat the other scores that they monitored from other teams' early meets—which determined their level of risk. And at every step, the gymnasts looked to add a skill that could boost their chances of a high score without making it too difficult and sacrificing a score due to a mistake instead. This was where being so closely tied to Gym World came in handy: Leah and Maria were responsible for carrying on the streak, but in practice, they saw the gymnasts only a few times a week at high school events where they could gauge their progress. Most of the gymnasts practiced the other days of the week with their club coaches. So, if they got a tougher skill reliably down in club practice, the club coach would quickly relay to the high school coaches that it might be a good idea to try in the high school routine.

At meets, a routine's start value depended on its difficulty.

"We fight this battle of if is it worth getting that one extra tenth of a point instead of starting at a 9.9, or start at 10 to not lose that one-tenth, but then also have that risk of falling on that skill or getting more execution off on that skill," Leah said. "For example, if it's a leap pass on floor and you're not hitting 180, they're going to take probably two-tenths on that. So you gain that start value, but then you still get two-tenths taken off. So it is a very big math problem."

The year before, after the sectionals meet, the coaches decided their goal score for state meet was 150. It would have beaten a Bees record of 149.9, which was set by the 2005 team and for that team, with three seniors who had three years of experience competing in the state meet, it seemed reasonable, even though they fell short. But this year was different. This year, the coaches didn't know what level any of the gymnasts could step up to—it was the youngest team they had in a long time. But they knew it would be closer to 147, if they could even get there—the first two meets had been well under that.

They also didn't even have their full team practicing due to commitments to their club team. One of the biggest factors in the math equation was GG, a sophomore and a level 10 club gymnast who hadn't competed for the team yet. She would return next week, in the fifth regular season meet of the season, the Beauty and the Beast. But they weren't sure how many points she would add.

"I think I'm very confident in her vault and floor and I'm very confident in my whole team on vault and floor," Leah said. "Those have always been really good events for us, which used to set us apart. But now for a lot of teams, those are also very good events. So Brunswick, for example, they're very, very good on vaults. They have a powerhouse vaulting team and [the] same with floor. So once I started to notice in the last few years that beam and bars is what really sets a winning team apart, that's where I started to steer more of my emphasis on those two events."

"GG, last season, took fourth in the all-around in the individual state meet, with a first-place finish in the vault. But she wasn't a powerhouse on beam and bars, at least not as a freshman. And she's my lead competitor," Leah said.

. . .

The high school team's most important team practice was the one held with the full team each weekend—it was one of the few times they were all together as a team, but there was limited time to work on individual skills because there were so many gymnasts. To make the practices more interesting and motivate the team, each weekend practice included some sort of competition between two equally divided groups.

The night before a practice in January, the team captains, Ella and Delaney, were tasked with getting their teams ready for the practice. They started text chains specifying what face paint should be applied, ribbon colors and more. Delaney was in charge of Team Rock (theme: neon) and Ella was captain of Team Blackout (colors: red and gold). Thanks to years of competing in gymnastics, all Brecksville gymnasts easily had a part of a closet somewhere in their house filled with the very supplies meant exactly for occasions like this.

The gymnasts showed up ready to compete—full makeup, full hair, full paint, full matching ribbons.

The groups alternated between the four events, just like a real meet. GG sat in the middle of the gym and helped keep the score. "I think we're doing good," she said. "We're getting better scores every meet."

Once the mock meet started, the group was energized. When a Brecksville-Broadview Heights gymnast competed in a meet, her teammates sat in a semicircle or line watching and cheering their loudest. And in practice, they replicated the atmosphere perfectly—part of the reason coaches required this was to motivate them and part was to get them used to the noise that they'd hear when they're competing.

With Team Rock competing on bars, the cheers for bar routines followed the same pattern. For example, for Jeanne, it started with her teammates yelling a firm "Let's go, Jeanne!" as she jumped up and started her routine. Then with every move, turn, or grip change, the cheers grew a little louder. It almost sounded like a group trying to will with their cheers for the gymnast to stay on. "Let's GO, Jeanne!" Another move. "Let's go, Jeanne." "You got it!" "YES JEANNE!" And then the dismount and a collective and uniform sigh of relief. "Yayyyyy!"

Then immediately, it started again for the next gymnast. "Come on, Delaney," they shouted at the senior captain. "Let's go, Delaney." And the same cadence continued on.

Amid the cheers for the uneven bars, Leah noticed that it seemed quiet on the side of the gym. "Red team," she shouted. "Are we alive over there?"

She increased the volume in her voice to as loud as she could.

"LET'S GO."

From her perch next to the balance beam, Joan sighed.

"Why is everyone frowning?" she shouted.

At club practices, Joan sat next to the balance beam—that was her area of focus. At this moment, her goal was to make sure that the gymnasts tightened up the little things that could cost fractions of a point. And that could be things as simple as forgetting to smile during the routine. Or an errant step or angle. "That's not going to make a difference in club gymnastics," she pointed out, "but for high school, tenths of a point added together could mean a lot."

She looked again over at Emily doing her floor routine with a frown that was often her default expression when she was concentrating.

"Positive attitude!" Joan yelled. "Come on, Emily, light that thing up."

Later in the practice, once the group got to the vault, the coaches' mood improved.

Emily was the first to earn Leah's praise with her vault as she completed her Yurchenko, a type of vault named for the gymnast Natalia Yurchenko, where a gymnast starts with a roundoff onto the springboard and then does a back handspring onto the vault table. (The level of difficulty can increase depending on what happens after that—Simone Biles, for example, competed a Yurchenko Double Pike, the most difficult vault in women's gymnastics.)

"That was a 9.5, 9.6 vault," Leah said of Emily's vault. "Holy cow, I'm so excited, Emily."

The energizing performances kept coming.

"Whew, 50 points for Ella because she just landed a Kas," Maria added after the senior landed a vault that started with a Kas, a roundoff with a half turn onto the table. For Ella, this was a big deal. Adding a Kas—named for the Japanese gymnast Shigeru Kasamatsu—would increase her start value on vault from a 9.7 to a 10.0. Since she was currently slated to be one of the six competitors, this was especially important. For the state meet, especially, that could be a difference-maker.

Rachel took that to heart. Something about the mock meets turned on every competitive fiber in her body and she wanted to do everything she could to make her team win. When it was her turn on the vault, she started negotiating. She was on Delaney's team and she was going to be sure they won this meet. If the Kas had been 50 points," she asked aloud, "could a different skill add 25?"

The coaches didn't answer. She gave up and went back to practice.

It turned out Maria was about to pull off the biggest skill of all.

"I figured out the music," Maria yelled from the floor competition, where she had been struggling to put on the correct songs to match the routines all morning.

"50 points for Schneidy," one of the gymnasts responded.

Once the practice meet was complete and the score was tallied, Ella's team celebrated the win, which didn't actually mean anything. "I think we get first serve at team dinner or something," she said. They hadn't really been motivated by the thought of prizes or bragging rights. For both teams the energy at practice had changed the mood overall. And with the season getting closer to the state meet than the start of the season mark, they knew they needed to stay at that level.

It was a good practice.

But it wasn't perfect. It was far from perfect.

Leah stood on the mat with the gymnasts circled around her.

"Each week your routine should get easier. They look easy right now. Now we have to keep cleaning them up. Every single practice we have to take seriously, we have to hit the ground running. When GG comes back, we have three meets and postseason. It's already almost over. So these next three weeks, these next four weeks really matter.

"Every single practice you have to be at, there's no more missing practice."

"Well, they can't," interjected Maria, reminding them of the strict team rules about missing practice that she had laid out at the start of the season.

"You cannot do that," Leah continued. "All these other teams, I bet you not one kid is missing practice. Only time you miss practice is if you're throwing up or have COVID. Or some extreme family emergency. Other than that, you have to be here. Get your homework done on the weekends. Get off your phones, get off TikTok, get your homework done. Study, study, study. You're a student first and then an athlete. Take care of your bodies. Every single team day should look like this. If we have to play this every single team day, I will do it."

Leah continued.

"This is what I need. The way that you guys cheered for each other today was amazing. Every single meet should be like that. Every practice should be like that—club or high school. You've got to cheer for each other. You only got each other. So be there.

"But seriously, every single thing moving forward from here on out is going to be tough. Every little tenth matters. Every step. Dismount, even in practice. Our handstands on bars were so much better today. You have to continue to do that. Hold yourself to a high standard.

'Cause if you don't, this team's going to collapse. If every single person does their part, it's going to be easy. There were some good scores out there yesterday. We can do that, no problem. But it has to be this every single day at minimum. And then getting better each and every week. You should be able to do these routines in your sleep. Every single girl should be putting up 9.1s. We're there, we have it. They look for clean routines, dismounts."

The team got their stretches in and wandered off in groups. They were energized as they walked off into the cold and gray Cleveland January afternoon. "I feel like it was really good," Ella said as she walked out. "We haven't had a practice this good in a while, and I feel like everyone was confident in hitting all their stuff and getting a lot done, which I think is the most important thing."

The coaches were relieved and happy. Especially about Rachel. Rachel looked happier and more confident than she had in weeks.

It was getting there.

But it wasn't there yet.

The next meet would be at Lakewood and was marked as a chance for some of the gymnasts who didn't get to compete in many events to have their turn. Then the Beauty and the Beast meet at home, which was Senior Night and finally a home meet against Avon, which was the last meet before the Suburban League Championship, the first postseason meet.

It was still early in the season. But postseason was coming quickly.

CHAPTER 8

That School in Columbus

One hundred and thirteen miles away from Gym World, Jen Hedrick had stood in front of her team at Delaware Olentangy Berlin high school at the start of the season with a goal: Finish top three, they decided.

Jen was a high school gymnast when Brecksville won its first state title in 1994 and grew up knowing about the program. She was coaching at another school in the area when Olentangy Berlin was looking for a coach for their new program. Since she lived and taught elementary school in the district and had plans to send her daughters to that school, it was an easy choice.

Olentangy Berlin finished sixth in the state meet in 2022, so coming into the 2022–23 season, Jen had a goal for her gymnasts—to finish in the top three in the state. She figured with a few solid new additions, plus building on last year's team, they had a shot.

"My assistant looked at me like I was crazy," she said. "I did not think I was, I thought that that was, it was very doable to be in the top three. I knew we were gonna have to work for it, but I definitely thought it was something that was in our reach."

The private gyms that the gymnasts competed at in Berlin were a little different than the ones in the Cleveland area, which did allow club gymnasts to compete in high school: Gymnasts were allowed to compete in club, but more of a stepped-down program instead of the most competitive ones. So Jen's team was filled with gymnasts who loved gymnastics—and were solid competitors—but in many cases had just gotten burned out or didn't want to continue with the elite competition.

Junior Alex Downing competed at level 10 in club gymnastics in 2020, but then switched to high school. Stephanie Balthasar, a senior, had competed in high club-level gymnastics when she decided to switch to the high school team. Tia Estrada had competed in the individual day of state meet the year before, coming in sixth on bars. Freshman Tayten Swain had taken a hiatus from the sport before high school, but as a newspaper article in her high school paper said, she "reignited her love for the sport" when she joined the high school team.

She added to the paper that she was enjoying the team's "foundation and family atmosphere."

Before Tayten joined the team, Jen heard about her through the best kind of grapevine: secondhand gossip from her son.

"She had done competitive gymnastics, competed at level 9 or maybe level 10. She started gymnastics when she was three, trained about thirty hours a week," Jen said.

Then COVID hit.

And Tayten, who was competing at a high level in the seventh grade, was taking a break from gymnastics.

"It just so happened that I had a neighbor boy that was dating her," Jen said.

"And, so my son and the neighbor boy knew that I was a gymnastics coach and they kept telling me that I needed to meet this Tayten girl because she was so good."

Jen met her and told her to just come try out at the high school and hang out in the gym with the team. "No pressure," she said. "I don't care if you do anything."

Slowly, Tayten started to come into the gym and work out. "I just was happy to see her in the gym and if she wanted instruction I gave it, but it was more to just kind of let her play and get back on the equipment," Jen said.

That's Jen's whole philosophy as a coach: High school gymnastics, she strongly believed, was supposed to be fun. "I'm just more about, I want you to love the sport of gymnastics and I want you to be the best that you can be," she said. And that's how, she said, she coached. No yelling, just encouragement and enthusiasm.

But, of course, she wanted her team to do well.

Olentangy Berlin also had some depth at vault with four strong vaulters, including her daughter, Kylie.

So, she knew that they could be in a good spot. But it wasn't until after the second meet that she had any idea of just how good.

In the first week of January, at the McGee Invitational, their second meet of the season, Olentangy scored a 146.575. Jen metaphorically looked around the state. Brecksville, so far in the numbers they had put out that season, hovered around a 142. And that invitational wasn't even Olentangy Berlin's best lineup. "I wanted to keep people healthy," Jen said.

The season still had weeks left in it—and judging, of course, wasn't the same across meets. But as Jen looked over to Cleveland, she couldn't help but notice that they were scoring much higher than the usual top three teams.

And she knew: Top three wasn't so much of a stretch after all.

Watching from only clips they could get on their phone and relying on the scouting reports from anyone they knew who had seen Olentangy Berlin, Maria and Leah knew it too.

. . .

Meanwhile, closer to Brecksville-Broadview Heights, the coaches at Brunswick—Christina Lenny and Jackie George—came in with the mindset they had: It's anyone's game. Christina and Jackie were both former Brecksville gymnasts—they were teammates and after Jackie started coaching at Brunswick, a high school twenty minutes west of Brecksville, she asked Christina to join.

Christina started at Gym World when she was in elementary school, after her family moved to the area from Florida. She stayed through winning the four state titles with the high school to start the state win streak before going on to compete at the Ganims' alma mater, Kent State. She was a three-time All-MAC team award winner there and led Kent State to its first NCAA Women's Gymnastics championship appearance. Like many gymnasts, she saw the Ganims as second parent-type figures, and when she was inducted into the Kent State Athletics Hall of Fame, she asked Joan to come with her. "I wouldn't have felt right going to that without having her there because she and

Mr. G were huge in my life. They had a huge impact, not only in my gymnastics career, but just in my entire life in general. Along with my parents, which is why I called them my second parents. They helped kind of shape me into the person who I am today," she said.

A picture of Christina hung in the office area of Gym World.

"They're just amazing," Christina added of the Ganims. "They're inclusive for everybody. If ever you need anything, no matter what it is, whether it's advice or a shoulder to cry on, they were always there."

Sometimes, she said, when she was training at Gym World, she wouldn't even have to say anything. Ron Ganim would just know something was wrong. "He'd pull me aside and ask, 'Are you okay? Is everything okay?'

"I'm so thankful for them and everything that they have done for me," Christina added. "Even as an adult, I'm just so grateful for them."

Christina loved competing for Brecksville—some of her favorite memories were team sleepovers, where they would paint shirts with puffy paint (something she lamented this generation of gymnasts would never understand). She loved the camaraderie of the team and the excitement of meets. She, of course, loved winning the state meet and credited the Ganims and Gym World club coaches for her winning the all-around.

And she loved high school gymnastics.

It's just, she thought, so much fun.

"I think there's a lot of stigma with high school gymnastics, but I think a lot of kids are realizing yeah, maybe I'm not going to do college gymnastics. Maybe let's try this. And they end up having so much fun. We had this girl for her first three years of high school; we were trying to get her to do high school gymnastics. We told her, you're going to have so much fun. You're going to love it.' But because [her club] coaches were saying, well no, you can't do it or you can't do both or you have to make a decision or it's not very competitive or whatever the case may be, she didn't do it. But then her senior year she goes, I'm going to try this. You know, it's my last year I'm not doing college gymnastics.

"And then she did it and she said, this is so much more fun. And then she essentially regretted not doing it the last three years. And I've heard that from a number of kids who have done it and they say, this is so much fun. I can't wait for next year."

But Christina and Jackie, key members of the inaugural wins of Brecksville's unprecedented win streak, wanted nothing more than to be responsible for the end of it. After all, they reasoned, that's why we're all here, right? To try to win the state meet?

"I mean it's all a friendly rivalry, at least for me in my perspective," Christina said. "Because everybody goes out when they compete, they want to win, they want to beat everybody. They want to come out on top. But the reality is there's only one winner. There's only ever going to be one winner."

She and Jackie were aiming for that—this year—to be them.

"Every year, I tell Mrs. G, 'You guys better watch it because we're coming for you. We're working, we want the title, we're coming for it.' And every single time she tells me the same thing: She goes, 'You know what Lenny, I wouldn't have it any other way.'"

Like Brecksville, Brunswick had a young team, but they had some stars returning. Bree Vargo, a sophomore, was a level 10 gymnast. Lauren Eyssen, a sophomore, finished third on the uneven parallel bars and tied for fifth on the vault at the individual day of the state meet the year before. Another gymnast, Alaina Timko, placed fourth on the beam on the individual day of the state meet.

They were a good team, Christina thought.

And like Olentangy Berlin, the McGee Invitational in early January had her thinking that this could be the year. Their score, a 145.425—far higher than Brecksville's that week—didn't go unnoticed by the Brecksville coaches or the gymnasts, who began wondering if they should go get a look at this team and see just how good they were.

. . .

Brecksville was also keeping an eye on Medina, whose mascot was the same as Brecksville-Broadview Heights—the Bees. The Medina coaches had ties to Gym World and were friendly with Joan, Leah, and Maria, but after last year's state meet, they couldn't forget the threat they posed. Medina, also, compared to the rest of the teams at the top, had a lot of upperclassmen—three seniors—Colleen Johnson, Macy Maxworthy, and Maddy Todorovich, who had all competed at state meet last year.

And by the first week of January, there were even more teams to watch: Hudson, which had come in fifth in 2022, had a 140 by the last week in December in a meet.

The thing about high school gymnastics, as every coach would say, was that even if a team was capable of a good score—a championship-winning one—it all depended on the day, which meant that with so many teams close to Brecksville's score, all it could take was a few falls or a few unexpected skills added at the last minute and executed to determine the champion.

. . .

If one gymnast could somehow topple the streak, the Ganims would have had a front-row seat to see the gymnasts who were going to beat them. Tessa Brousek, a sophomore, was part of the Padua Franciscan High School team that, like Brecksville, was coached by Leah. Padua was in a different conference than Brecksville-Broadview Heights—they're a Catholic school located in Parma, about a fifteen-minute drive from Brecksville (and where Ron grew up). They competed in the Crown Conference, which was the conference of Catholic schools in the greater Cleveland area, while Brecksville competed in the Suburban League. The only time they would go up against each other was in the district, sectional and state meets in postseason. The Brecksville coaches also coached Revere High School, twenty minutes away from Brecksville. Two gymnasts at that high school who competed for Gym World had been envious of the high school experience they saw many of their friends having and convinced the Revere athletic director, Don Seeker, to start a team there that year. Seeker, according to the high school student newspaper, happened to be friends with the Ganim family and called and asked if they would coach the team. Of course, they said yes.

For all training purposes—at least during team days—they operated as one. The Padua and Revere girls came to Gym World for practice and developed friendships with the Brecksville gymnasts. Joan, Maria, and Leah would all offer encouragement, coaching, and tips even if Leah was the official coach of the team.

Tessa had, then in middle school, been on the path of Junior Olympics and elite gymnasts. She attended school on a flexible schedule to accommodate her training. "I was on fast track to international assignments and all that stuff," she said. "But what really changed my mind was I really missed school and I missed my friends. I really wanted to get back to having fun in the sport and not seeing it as much of a job almost—that's kind of what I saw it as."

So she went back to school full time in the middle of seventh grade and competed at the top club level at Five Star Gymnastics, another club in the Cleveland suburbs, where she trained year-round. But going into her sophomore year, she was ready to try something different.

Tessa had an Achilles and back injuries in her career. But her worst injury, a concussion she suffered during her freshman year of high school, kept her sidelined for months from school and meets. "I was out for the majority of the season. So once I got back from that, it was a pretty slow recovery."

She spent a lot of time in concussion therapy to heal from the injury, and the process gave her some time to figure out what she wanted to do. And that, she decided, was high school gymnastics.

"I've always wanted to do high school," she said. "I thought it would be very exciting and my cousin did it and she said it's so much fun, you need to try it."

Tessa didn't want to get too far in high school and regret not giving it a shot.

"I talked to Leah last year before going into this season and she said, 'We'd love to have you on the team.'"

Something about Leah convinced her this was the right decision. She was sold. She joined Padua, limiting her training to Five Star to two days a week. She figured she was only a sophomore and if she ended up wanting to compete in college in gymnastics, Leah would be a good enough coach to get her there.

During the first practice, lining up with the Brecksville gymnasts—all of whom had known each other since they were little kids—Tessa was a bit nervous. But, she said, they went out of their way to welcome her and the rest of the Padua and Revere gymnasts. She said she felt her nervousness melt away. "I feel with Revere, Padua, and Brecksville, we're all kind of one team," she said. "We all compete for different schools, but we all support each other the same and from the first day Leah said,

'You guys are on one team and you have to cheer for each other and you guys have to make it known that you guys support each other.'"

Be loud, Leah and Maria would tell them. Have fun.

Tessa knew of Brecksville's state win streak coming in—at least vaguely. But now that she practiced so closely with them, she knew that even if they were treated by their coaches as one team, the thing that would separate them is that the Brecksville girls had a goal that Padua and Revere didn't have a big enough team to go after: a state title, much less one that added to a nineteen-year win streak, at least as a team.

From the start of the season, it was clear that Tessa was in another league.

In her season opening meet, she was the all-around winner, coming in first in vault, floor, and bars.

"I just felt a lot more confident than I ever did in club and I think as the season went on, the score started to reflect it even more," she said.

Tessa's confidence only increased over the weeks. She was having trouble with her beam routine, and Leah and Maria helped her with visualization, mantras, and more mental exercises, which she thinks did more to stop her from slipping off the beam than anything else.

Tessa wasn't the only Padua gymnast with high scores to start the season. Sophomore Lexi Bryan came in second in the all-around, winning beam with a 9.1 score in an early meet. And junior Elyse Morrow hit a 9.1 on her floor routine—all solid scores that at some point could have been in the top four for Brecksville.

But even if they thought of themselves as one team, they were very much separated on the gymnastics score sheets. So Leah, Joan, and Maria could only watch Tessa take over the gym and shake their heads. It's not that they weren't happy or confident with their team. Or not happy for her individual success and renewed love of the sport. But Tessa could have been a difference maker with her scores.

If only she lived in Brecksville or Broadview Heights.

CHAPTER 9

GG Returns

The Bees opened the new year in mid-January with a meet in Lakewood, another school on the west side outside of Cleveland, against Strongsville, Lakewood, Nordonia, and Chardon. With the regular season coming to an end in a few weeks, Maria and Leah used it as a chance to form the rest of the lineup. It was becoming clear at this point that Ella, Rachel, and Emily were holding strong to the top spots. Jeanne, who missed the first two state meets of her career due to injuries, also seemed to be finding a spot in at least three events—bars (her strongest), beam, and floor. At Lakewood, Bailey finished first on beam, something that caught Leah and Maria's attention as they were trying to figure out what lineup could outperform last year's disaster. Bailey started the sport when she was in preschool. She had so much energy—running, tumbling, and jumping on everything—that her parents just wanted her to have an outlet. By middle school when she was doing Psychobabble at Gym World with Maria, she would hear stories about the high school team from her and Leah. "I want to be a part of that," she remembered thinking.

Bailey was thrilled to find herself performing well early in the season—she'd been regularly in the vault lineup and placed well in meets. She'd also started to hear some pointers from the coaches that seemed like she might have a chance at making the state lineup. And after the first meet, she didn't have the freshmen jitters that often came with joining any high school team, much less one expected to win the state title each year. "I came into the season pretty comfortable because I knew 90 percent of the girls already, because I've been training with them pretty much all my life," she said. "I didn't think it was as stressful for me because I knew everyone. I knew the coaches, but there was pressure just knowing we had to keep the streak going."

As January hit its second week, the deadlines passed for Delaney and Ella to send in their college applications. Ella, who had juvenile diabetes, hoped to be a surgical nurse one day. In an ideal world, she always thought she'd be a surgeon, but because of the problems that fluctuations in her blood sugar caused, she wasn't sure that would be possible. She applied to Ohio State, Cincinnati, Kentucky, Akron, West Virginia, and Minnesota. Delaney hoped to study chemical engineering. With college coming up, the seniors knew that their gymnastics careers in high school and in general were also coming to an end. The fifth meet of the year was a home meet, at Brecksville-Broadview Heights high school and was important for three reasons: It was Senior Night, it was an annual theme called Beauty and the Beast, and it was the first time that GG would be competing for the Bees.

Maria got the idea for Beauty and the Beast—now in its fifteenth season—after one of her gymnasts went on a college visit and reported back about the themed meet she saw on her visit. It paired a wrestling meet with a gymnastics meet with the idea that it would draw more of a crowd to both sports. It's been the source of puns and pithy article openers for local sportswriters following the team for years. In 2011 from the *Cleveland Plain Dealer*'s Tim Rogers's preview of the event: "The Beauty and the Beast is back and we're not talking the Broadway play or the Disney movie."

"It's a unique event in Ohio," then-athletic director Dan Kalinsky told Patch.com the year after. Beauty and the Beast meets continued to grow in popularity around college teams—Kent State, the Ganims' alma mater, hosted their first Beauty and the Beast in 2011. The University of Maryland, former Brecksville star Alecia Farina's alma mater, hosted it annually—the Maryland Terps held their first one in 2015.

Maria always wanted her gymnasts to get more recognition and the gymnasts agreed. Rachel raged one day the year before when she heard on the announcements that another team had won a game when on that same day, the Bees had won a postseason event that would put them on the road to another state title. Their win, according to her memory of the morning announcements, had been completely overlooked. Even if their friends did know about the high school gymnastics team and how good they were, Ella pointed out, they could never truly seem to grasp the history of the program. "They don't really understand all the pressure that's on us," she said. "They know, they're excited our school has the streak that we have. But they don't really know all the pressure and stuff that happens to us on the team." The meet was also an easy partnership—the wrestling coach, Todd Haverdill, was a longtime friend of Maria's and her former teaching partner. He now had two daughters on the team. This season the wrestling team was competitive—Todd was hoping to have two state championships in his house—one from his daughters, Lea and Kyla on the team, and one from his own team.

The night before the meet, the team set up the gym and had a team dinner at the school. Maria was excited. Todd had secured a tunnel and smoke machine to make the high schoolers' entrance memorable. "Thank you to all tonight!" she wrote in the parents' group chat. "Less than an hour to set up. Amazing. Tomorrow after meet we will take down and then girls will celebrate our two seniors with cake and dessert."

She added: "Tomorrow is going to be so much fun!"

On Instagram, Leah honored Delaney and Ella with posts highlighting their careers. "Delaney is a 4 year BEE and has been doing gymnastics from a young age. She is captain of the team this year and participated in Band and NHS outside of Gymnastics. Delaney competed for the BEES last year on Floor at the state meet and is a strong contender for line ups this year. Delaney we are so lucky to have you on our team the last 4 years! 🐝!! 😍 🥹"

For Ella: "Ella is a 4 year bee and has qualified in the all around to state meet the last 3 seasons! Ella is a major part of the success of the BEES the last 3 years, being runner up on bars in 2021! Ella is also a member of the band and NHS. Ella we are so proud of the athlete and person you have become! We are BEEyond lucky to have you!"

On Ella's post, they added another important request for anyone who might be reading: "COME SUPPORT TONIGHT AT BBHHS AT 6 pm!!!"

It would just be awesome, they all thought, if they could have a packed house to show off in front of before the postseason.

. . .

While the focus was on the seniors, GG, a sophomore, had been waiting for weeks to hear her name in the lineup. She kept score in practice mock meets, dutifully cheered on her teammates, and heard her coaches point to the before of the season (when she was still focused on her club routine) and the after (when she joined and the squad was complete) and close to the postseason. GG is one of, if not the, shortest gymnasts on the team with her long light brown hair tied into a bun during meets. She's a twin—Alexa, her twin sister, was a cheerleader whom their parents described as the outgoing and louder one. GG was reserved and quiet until she knew you and generally outwardly calm at all times—even in high-pressure situations—a quality her mom said came from her dad. "I'm a steady Eddie," her dad Joe said, which meant, he said, that it was hard to tell how the meet went when looking at GG's demeanor after an event. "She can win the meet, calm. She can lose the meet, calm. You never know. I mean, you would never know unless you ask her because she doesn't get high high or low low. But I think that's important . . . you have to take care of your business. She's very practical about it," he said.

GG's parents, Joe and Alicia, ran an optometry practice in Brecksville. "Ron and Joan [Ganim] were patients of ours before we ever had children," Joe said. When GG and Alexa were five or six, their parents took them to Gym World to try it out—along with Cheer World. "They both went and Joan watched them flip," Joe remembered. She quickly assessed their strengths and Alexa was sent to the cheerleader gym. GG went to Gym World.

The two gyms were next door to each other, which made it convenient for Joe and Alicia. "One goes this way, one goes that way and there you go," Joe said. "That's how we got them into it. And we knew we wanted them to be in something because keep them active when they're young and we have two of them." The Ravagnanis also had a son, who was five years older than the twins. GG quickly took to the sport and by the time she was in eighth grade, her parents remembered her anticipation of joining the high school team. "The girls were already talking 'next year when Gianna's here,'" her dad remembered.

Maria, when responding to an email for a preview in the local paper before GG had competed in a single meet, wrote that she hoped

GG would take the spot of a graduating senior who had been the vault champion the year before—a tall order for a freshman. Maria had almost been too worried to hope for this. Before the 2022–23 season, GG was described in Cleveland.com as "the future of Brecksville gymnastics."

"The sky is the limit for this bright Bee who is soaking up every moment of her early career," reporter Robert Fenbers wrote.

"She is a pistol," Maria told the reporter. "She is so good. She just loved high school gymnastics. She loved the experience. She can't wait for the season to start this year. She continues to get better and improve with her skills and hopes to get the same result this year, with even more consistency."

GG and her family had something else important to the team as a whole—a large finished basement perfect for team dinners and hangouts and big enough to fit the nearly two dozen teenagers. As sophomore parents, Joe and Alicia knew the drill: They bought pizza, snacks, put them in the basement and made themselves scarce upstairs. During the team bonding, the gymnasts took turns singing karaoke songs—the sound floated lightly upstairs to where Joe and Alicia could hear them. Rachel, many of her teammates agreed, was the best karaoke performer on the team, belting out an impressive version of the Miley Cyrus song "Party in the USA," willing to be goofy and put herself fully into the song. (Other team choices included Carrie Underwood's "Before He Cheats" and Justin Bieber jams from early in his career.)

GG was held out of the high school meets and practices because she was focused on club—performing well in a meet to qualify for the club state meet, which is how she would get to nationals at the club level. The year before she had made nationals as an alternate. This year, she hoped to get a spot in nationals again—and the road to that with her club coaches at Gym World was what delayed her high school season start. While it may have been marked as a point in the season by the coaches, it wasn't rare for some of the better gymnasts to take longer to join the team in a full capacity. Ohio State High School Athletic Association rules said that gymnasts must cease noninterscholastic gymnastics competition six weeks (forty-two days) prior to the Monday of the week of the state tournament in gymnastics, in order to be eligible for OHSAA tournament competition.

So GG competed for her club on January 10, 2023, in the Battle of the Champions in Toledo. She took first in vault in her division. Nine days later, she and the rest of the Bees walked into the Beauty and the Beast meet under a large red arch with the gold words "Go Bees" and a cartoonish-looking Bee on top of it. The gym was packed, as they had hoped. Some of them walked arm in arm with members of the wrestling team, but most of them just poured out of the entrance—complete with smoke around them coming from the smoke machine Todd had brought to the gym for effect. GG walked out in her warm-ups with the fanfare directed more at the seniors and made her high school season debut. She took first in bars and floor and third in vault and all-around. It felt good to be with her team again—after weeks of watching, she was ready to contribute.

In addition to GG's strong return at the Beauty and the Beast meet, Rachel took second on floor exercise and Emily came in third on beam. The lineups were looking more clear. "One more meet til conference and then postseason!" Leah wrote on the Instagram account. "#just-rock."

. . .

Even though Rachel had taken second on floor exercise, her mental blocks were getting worse. It started with vault. She was warming up weeks earlier when she realized: "I can't do this." She went and told Leah and Maria. But then, her brain had moved onto another block: a pass in her floor routine. She told her coaches again and instead completed a watered-down routine—good enough for a regular-season meet, but trouble for the postseason.

In her floor exercise, Rachel had started to hold herself back on her pass, which was supposed to be a roundoff whip half-front pike. "I was having trouble with the twisting part," she said.

As with her more skilled vault, her brain started telling her that she couldn't do it. "I don't really think I can do this," she thought. "I don't really want to do this."

Even though the Ganims and Gym World may have been ahead of the curve when it came to mental training in gymnastics, none of it was guaranteed. A little more than a year before Rachel's latest troubles,

American gymnast Simone Biles—considered by many to be the best gymnast the sport has ever seen—dropped out of two 2021 Olympics finals events. She cited something called "twisties"—a type of mental block where gymnasts can't land safely even on routines and skills they've done for years. "I had no idea where I was in the air," Biles told reporters. "I could have hurt myself." It wasn't quite what Rachel had—hers was a fear of going backward on floor and in her vault—but the idea of a mental block was the same. And, of course, it's not just gymnastics where the mental part of the sport could be the toughest. In baseball, the yips were blamed for the sudden inability to accurately throw a baseball, no matter how skilled the player. In golf, the yips caused involuntary wrist spasms that made even the best unable to putt. In 2017, Cavaliers player Kevin Love spoke about how he had a panic attack in the middle of a game—he sprinted into the locker room mid-game. As the mental side of sports continued to become a more prevalent problem, athletes were often granted a bit of understanding when they were facing them.

But Rachel wasn't a gymnast in the public eye getting supportive tweets or a professional baseball player or golfer able to open up to a friendly reporter about their struggles (though everyone on the professional level with mental blocks has also faced enormous backlash). She didn't get praised by LeBron James as Kevin Love had for sharing her struggles.

She was a fifteen-year-old high school gymnast who was supposed to be in four events with skills worth enough points to win a state championship and continue a streak that started before she was born. She was an integral part of the math to how her team got there this year.

And there was no way that even understanding what she was going through could make it better or give her another shot in the future.

Because the truth was, if she couldn't get it together, the streak could be over. She knew it. And her teammates knew it too. They were already in a rebuilding year after losing three of their top gymnasts. They saw her frustration in the gym during skills and would come over with something that she found almost as irritating as not being able to do the skill itself: "Come on," they told her. "You need to figure something out. You need to get this. You need to pull it together and stuff like that."

It was a common refrain in the team that was echoed throughout the year in different situations—a tough conditioning session, bad practice, someone struggling. "We can't lose states," they told each other. "We have to get it together because we can't lose states."

But it wasn't helping. Rachel didn't need to be reminded of the stakes. "You have to get it together," they repeated to her, "so we don't lose states."

She knew.

She'd been in this sort of funk before. But time was running out on the season. And she didn't know how to make it better.

CHAPTER 10

Taken for Granted

Todd Haverdill sat in the bleachers overlooking the gym floor at the Bees' final regular season meet of the year, with an eye trained on his middle daughter, Kyla, a freshman, as she warmed up on the bars a few feet away from his oldest daughter, Lea, a junior. The Brecksville wrestling coach since 2001, he won his own Ohio state championship as a high school wrestler for Lake Catholic. At twenty-three, he became the head coach at Brecksville, a job he once said in a podcast that he took almost by happenstance but hadn't left since.

He guided his Bees to a state championship in 2015 and six second-place finishes, and this year he thought they had a chance to go back to the top and add another championship banner to the wall. If it weren't for the gymnastics program, he would be the head of the most successful program at the high school and considered the best coach. He took the school's team from an average suburban program to a nationally ranked one.

Long before Kyla and Lea started gymnastics, he knew the Ganim family. In addition to working closely with Maria, as a young coach he asked Ron Ganim to speak to his team. He modeled some of the mental exercises he did with his team around Psychobabble—they spoke each week as a team about creating a winning culture. Around the time that Todd had started building the wrestling program at Brecksville, Lea started the toddler classes at Gym World. "They get involved, but it's just mommy and me class," he remembered. "And then it's rainbow class. And then the next thing you know, they're in high school. They joke because wrestling's like a cult too. And I always say for gymnastics, once you're in, you can't get out."

He and his wife Melissa, who played soccer in college, tried other sports with Lea. T-ball. Soccer. Tennis. But nothing stuck like gymnastics.

Todd looked over as Kyla continued to warm up on the floor. He knew how tough it was to win a state title, and even tougher to win as many as they had in a row when Lea joined the team as a freshman. "I think the pressure is very real. [As a parent] I'm thinking of two things, right? Number one, I thought that [state win] streak was just something super cool until my kids got on the team.

"And now I'm thinking, geez man, I don't want my kids to be on the team that doesn't win. Right? And so, not that there's pressure as a parent, I don't perform. I just want my kids to do well. I don't think my kids truly understand how special it is to be on a state championship team. Because it's always been that way.

"It's completely taken for granted here. It's just, 'Oh, they won again.' And that makes me sad, a little bit. I wish they could really truly understand. Not to make this about wrestling, but we were fortunate enough in 2015 to win the state title. And it was like, oh my God. Like we took down the world, right? It was the greatest moment. For them, it's just something that they do and they're expected to win and I don't know that they truly appreciate what's going on."

Kyla started gymnastics before she could walk—as a baby at the mommy and me classes at Gym World. She had known since about then too, she said, that she would be part of the high school team and was excited to watch when Lea kicked off her high school career two years earlier. Lea, likewise, was thrilled to have her on the team. Kyla stopped competing in club gymnastics before her ninth-grade season—she's on the soccer team as well and it was just too much to try to balance.

Kyla came in eager to help the team in any way that she could. It was something she'd looked forward to for most of her career—being a Bee. "My goal coming into freshman year was just to have a hard work ethic and to help the team in all the ways I can—if that's moving mats, any of that," she said. "And to be positive and help my teammates out because everyone has those mental breakdowns and stuff. I just want to be there for everyone and know that there's going to be a lot of that this season because there's a lot of pressure on us."

Even if Todd tried to explain to Kyla and Lea about the pressure to win the title, though, state championships, pressure, and the inner workings of the dynamics of the gymnastics team weren't normal dinner conversations in the house, which, Todd thought, was healthy. "A coaching philosophy for me is don't make things bigger than they are. In wrestling whether you're at the first match of the year or the last, somebody's going to win, somebody's going lose, and you do the best you can." Kyla and Lea, he said, came home and the conversation was just a simple one about how practice went and if anything hurt.

"It's 'Make sure you get your dinner and you get your homework done.' You know one of the things that I'm learning about gymnastics is they don't send out the lineup until the night before. And so to me, that's really interesting. In wrestling we know our lineup early in the week." So sometimes at dinner, he'd ask if they're competing in the meet. Usually the answer was that they don't know for sure. "But other than that, we don't talk about it at home. But I don't know that we talked about not talking about it at home."

They all just wordlessly agreed, it seemed, on his philosophy: Don't make it bigger than it's going to be.

There were, of course, the dad and coachisms that he did offer. If Lea or Kyla weren't competing, he reminded them to do what they can do to help the team. Hold a mat, take a video, hold up scores, things like that. "We'll talk about that kind of stuff a lot more, but not really about the *X*'s and *O*'s."

The day before this meet, though, that had changed a bit. It was a snow day and school was cancelled so the family went to lunch. With two members of the family on the team, the dynamic had changed a little bit—and the *X*'s and *O*'s were more prevalent in conversation.

"For probably the first time they were talking a little bit about what they thought the lineup at state might be," he said. "And I think that's the first time I've ever had a conversation about that with my kids."

For the gymnasts, it was impossible to really think about much else. This meet against Avon was the last one until the postseason, one of the few remaining chances to impress the coaches and secure a spot in the state meet. The next meet would be the conference championship, which was a point of pride but not impactful on the postseason. Then came sectionals, then districts, then—scores willing—states.

One of the biggest questions the coaches were focused on was the sixth spot in vault. Leah had it narrowed down to a few gymnasts, including Abby, the junior who had high hopes of grabbing one of the lineup spots.

Abby was one of the rare exceptions in the Brecksville-Broadview Heights group. Despite having grown up in the area, she started her gymnastics career at The Little Gym, a nationwide franchise of gyms. But she quickly switched to Gym World on the advice of a family friend, Beth Good, who had competed for the Brecksville-Broadview Heights High School team in the 1990s, including the 1994 team, which won the state meet.

"She used to always say 'Abby's so strong, she's fearless, you should put her in gymnastics, you should take her to Gym World,'" Abby's mom Janelle said. They were hesitant. They weren't sure if they wanted to get involved in gymnastics, but eventually they found themselves at Gym World.

The Gym World coaches immediately saw one thing—as Beth said, Abby was fearless. "She'd do whatever they told her to do and she was never nervous. She'd jump off high stuff and I think that was a big part of what they were looking for in a girl who could go far," Janelle remembered.

Abby competed at Gym World until a combination of the COVID-19 pandemic and injuries during her freshman year of high school made her rethink things. She decided to end her club gymnastics career and focus only on the high school team. It was a tough decision. It felt, on many levels, that she was giving up something when she gave up being part of the prestigious club program.

But three years later, Abby knew she had made the right decision. She was still on the best high school gymnastics team in the state and had time to pursue music, her real passion. She was about to start rehearsals for the high school musical, *Mean Girls* after the end of the gymnastics season. She also produced her own electronic music and had published some on the streaming service Spotify. She participated in chamber choir and planned on attending a five-week music camp in the summer. "I'm hoping to go to Berklee College of Music in Boston and do electronic production and design or a composition major of some sort," she said.

And she still, going into her junior year, was part of two state championship teams.

So when it came to everything that had happened since she quit the club team to focus on high school gymnastics, she came to a realization at some point. Instead of stepping down, "it took a while to recognize this, but I feel I've stepped up," she said.

Janelle said it was the best choice they could have made for her daughter's mental health as well. "Letting her step down from club allowed her to enjoy gymnastics more again," she said.

During Abby's freshman year, she hurt her ankle so wasn't able to compete at the state meet. In her sophomore year, she was an alternate. So now, in her junior year, she was hoping that she could find herself in the vault lineup at least for the state meet.

. . .

Maria, in addition to taking stock of where her team was days away from postseason, was dealing with an injury of her own and sitting down behind the scorer's table. Her back had always been a little sore from years of overuse from exercise and gymnastics. But then this week came an embarrassing accident. She fell down the steps and was sure she had slipped a disc. "Ever since then it's just felt terrible. But I'm having a cortisone shot on Monday. I'm hoping that will help," she said.

She looked over to the boys' section of the meet, where her youngest son Jimmy was competing. Her husband Bill had gotten roped into officiating at the last minute. Ohio's last varsity state meet for boys was in 1994—Mike Canales came in second in the all-around for the final individual meet—but the boys' varsity programs went dormant after that. When Maria's oldest son Joey was a freshman at Brecksville in 2019, she petitioned to bring back boys' gymnastics as a club sport. Similar to her mom's philosophy for the team back in the 1990s, she thought that the boys who trained in gymnastics for hours on end deserved some recognition. The team started with five freshmen and two seniors, all of whom had trained at Gym World. They mostly just competed against each other. Four years later, Joey was at college, but the club was still together, anchored by senior Blaise Rousseau, a Gym World gymnast who was likely to compete in college and his brother, Broc, another high-level gymnast who trained at Gym World.

But her focus was on her girls team and the list of roster possibilities she and Leah needed to start narrowing down. The season had gone by quickly, and finalizing the rosters for the final few meets of the season and the start of the postseason was tricky. It was more difficult than years before—the team was the biggest it had been in years and most of them were club gymnasts, meaning Maria and Leah saw them only once a week as a full team in practice. They had to rely on those impressions, meets, and what they heard from their club coaches about what skills they were developing in addition to the score averages from regular season meets. They were also monitoring how well the team was getting along and making sure there were no late-season problems. With a group of teenage girls, there were always bound to be a few interpersonal issues, especially stemming from stuff going on outside the gym.

Maria had a network of sources when it came to monitoring how the team was gelling outside of the gym. The team dinner, earlier that week, she said, had been at freshman Carol Samuel's house—and Carol's sister happened to be in Maria's health class. "She told me they were laughing and screaming until 9 or 10 at night," she said. "They're getting along just fine."

What she was anxious about was the lineups. She wanted to make sure that everyone was getting the best chance to show off their skills and compete for a spot in the lineup. She was anxious about beam. She felt fairly confident about the floor and vault lineups as long as everyone stayed healthy. She mostly felt good about bars. But what she was still most anxious about was the thing she couldn't control—other teams. For most of the schools that she thought could measure up, she would see them at least shortly before states in sectionals, districts, or even the conference tournament. Rachel, Lea, and some of the other gymnasts had even gone to meets of some of the top teams nearby to scout the competition. It was the first time she ever remembered having a group of gymnasts do that. But she was most nervous from watching the scores that continued to pop up from Olentangy. "I want to see what they have," she said.

To close out the regular season, the Bees beat Magnificat, Avon, and Padua. GG won the all-around with second on vault, bars, floor, and a third-place finish on beam. Ella took third in all-around, Emily took fourth in all-around and vault, and Rachel secured a fourth-place finish in floor (still competing in a watered-down routine). Jeanne finished fourth on beam.

Jeanne, tall with dark blonde hair, wore a back brace when she competed. Her parents moved to Broadview Heights from Pennsylvania for her dad's job when she was in elementary school. In the interview process, her mom Addie remembers, her husband Uwe was asked if he had any kids and their interests. When he mentioned that Jeanne was into gymnastics, Uwe's future coworker smiled. They were in the right place for that.

Quickly, Jeanne was in the competitive track at Gym World, but her career was marred with injuries. She broke an ankle in elementary school. She had a bad concussion that sidelined her for a season. ("We were doing double backs on trampoline and I just completely over-rotated and smacked my head. And I got whiplash. That sucked.")

In middle school, she started having back issues, which at first she just thought was an overuse issue. But then one day, it felt a lot worse. "I snapped back in an arch and that's when I said, 'Oh shoot. That really hurt,'" she said.

The pain continued for about a year and she missed a lot of training. She went to physical therapy and took breaks from the sport. Two different spinal injections meant to help the pain didn't work. They made it worse. "I can't keep doing this," she thought of the sport.

Her parents were lost. "We had gone through and basically exhausted physical therapy," Addie remembered. "We were seeing a medical doctor for that. She was the chair of sports medicine and she ended up sending us to one of her partners who was an osteopathic doctor because she said they do more hands-on manipulations and things like that." Jeanne still wasn't getting better. "We did that for a few months and that was incredibly painful. And then at that point, I think I thought, okay, let's maybe get another opinion. Let's take her to a back specialist, let's look outside of sports medicine just to see if there's something that we're missing."

Still, there was no diagnosis. "Almost every time we would almost hope somebody would find something on an X-ray or on an MRI, because then they might be able to say this is what this is, and you'll get better in eight weeks," Addie said. "And that never happened. There was no finite end to this problem."

It wasn't just gymnastics. Sitting too long in school without getting up to walk around was tough for Jeanne. Finally, in seventh grade, a doctor diagnosed Jeanne with a chronic pain condition, one that made her reflexes misfire and identify something as pain even if it wasn't something that should have sparked that protective reflex. Soon after, she went to an intensive program at Cleveland Clinic that worked to rehab children experiencing chronic pain.

Jeanne took three weeks off school and her regular life to enter the program at the hospital. It was outpatient, though many of the participants, some of whom had come from hours away, slept at the hospital. "One girl, she would have seizures all the time so she was in there for that," Jeanne remembered. "And then there were other people with back problems from different sports and so we were all doing kind of the same thing, trying to figure out how to get the pain to stop."

There was a classroom, where the patients would try to keep up with their schoolwork. But no gymnastics, no regular school, nothing outside of the program and home. It was a series of long days in the hospital.

It was a weird time. She remembered the last day of practice before she entered the program. Despite the pain she was in, she tried to savor that time with her friends. She wouldn't see them, it seemed then, for a long time.

They had a psychologist at the hospital to talk with about the intensity of everything that was happening. They did water therapy.

And when the program was over, Jeanne felt . . . better. She decided she wanted to keep doing gymnastics.

"I think I've just always loved it and I didn't want to give up on it if there was a way that I could keep doing it," she said. "I just wanted to find a way to be able to keep doing it."

Now, more than three years later, Jeanne still went to the hospital once a week for physical therapy. She also volunteered there—and planned on studying something in the medical field in college (she wanted to go to a big college somewhere warm). She thought it would be easy for her to relate to her patients.

"I'd be able to say, oh yeah, that happened to me too," she thought of her future patients.

The pain wasn't totally healed—and it didn't start or stop with her back. "Most recently my shoulder decided to start hurting from the new bar routine I was doing," she said.

It seemed, at times, beyond understanding to keep going. "I love the sport," Jeanne explained. She loved getting new skills and conquering a challenge that was difficult. She loved being part of the team. She loved challenging herself. She couldn't imagine her life without it, especially in the moments when she mastered a new routine. "Because even though it hurts when you're doing that, you don't think about the pain.

"You're just thinking, oh I love this."

This season, Jeanne knew that the coaches were counting on her—the constant refrain to not get hurt started in the offseason when she had Joan as her coach for summer gymnastics. "Jeanne, don't overdo it," she would tell her. "We need you to compete this season. If it hurts, stop doing it." She was doing well in practice and competition on bars, where she was constantly tweaking her routine and beam, where she had an important ritual before getting on the beam. It was one that Maria had given her. "I," she said out loud right before she competed, "Am good at beam."

Beam, she said, always made her the most nervous. "I know I can do it. So when I'm doing it, I just tell myself I can do it. Or I think about the little parts of the skill instead of just thinking 'don't fall.'"

Because of her injuries, Jeanne didn't compete in vault. Leah told her that they didn't need her in that event and they would rather her not injure herself again. But she was hopeful that she would be competing in the other three events—beam, bars, and floor at states. Even though Leah and Maria didn't tell the gymnasts the lineups beforehand, the gymnasts, Jeanne said, could get a pretty good idea of where they stood. "Once you have a couple of good meets, you kind of figure out, 'Oh, I might be ending up here or in this part of the lineup.'" There are also hints that the gymnasts pick up from what Leah and Maria tell them at practice that they might be in consideration.

And even though they were all competing against each other for a spot, Jeanne thought this team got along well—not only with each other but the Padua and Revere gymnasts who practiced with them. They'd always gotten the message that team comes first over any personal drama. "I feel like we've always been a good team. We all see each other every day. We all know each other really well and we're all there to support each other during each other's routines. With my bar routine, everybody was giving me pep talks before I went.

"It's a good feeling to be a part of the team and I think it's always been like that." It was also helpful, she said, the older they got, the longer they'd known each other, which for many of them at this point, was nearly a decade. Freshman Brooke Smerdel said a lot of that closeness on the team, even for the girls who hadn't been on the team years before, stemmed from how Jeanne made sure they were all brought into the circle. "She's a big sister to all of us," she said. "She is just very inclusive to all of us and [makes] sure none of us were left out just because we were lowerclassmen and makes sure she is always there for everyone."

Brecksville scored a 145.1 in its final win of the regular season. That was still 1.5 points less than Berlin Olentangy had scored to start the month. And it was three tenths of a point lower than Medina, the team that came in second in the 2022 state meet, had scored in their latest meet.

Thinking about the discrepancy between where the team was at this point last year, and comparing them to other teams, Leah shrugged. "It's kind of where we're at," she admitted. "It doesn't give us as much cushion as I've had in previous seasons. Looking at last year's conference meet, we scored 149, which is huge, but I also had three seniors that contributed to the constant 9.3, 9.4, 9.5 scores. This year with a lot of younger freshmen and sophomores, I just don't have that precision as I did with my seniors, which that'll come in time."

There were also a number of meets she pointed to where the team had to count falls or other mistakes that could be cleaned up or avoided in the postseason.

Leah thought about that a lot. The difference between a perfect meet and a bad one and the blurry space in between. She thought about it from the state meet the year before, when she saw her gymnasts deflated from mistakes—mistakes that could have been less egregious with a bit of resilience.

"I never expect a perfect meet," she said. "I just always expect a fight. And I think from the beginning of this year, I really decided to focus more on teaching the girls how to fight for their routines instead of giving up because I know, for example, that's just been an issue in the past of girls jumping off the beam on something that they could have saved."

And that focus, she thought, was why they were closer to their goal—which this year was still 147—than meet scores may have indicated.

"That was my huge goal going into this year," she continued. "You're going to fight for every single routine that you do. I don't care if you wobble 600 times, you're going to fight to stay on that beam and we can only get better from there. So that's something that all of the girls this year from the first meet on have really fought for, which I think is paying off this point of the season because now their routines are easy, which, at the beginning of the year, they weren't. So of course I expect them to make some mistakes, but now those mistakes are slowly going away."

Leah was thinking of small improvements at this point.

"I'm definitely looking for just cleanliness and confidence. Really honing in on hitting handstands on bars, stuck landings on beam and bars specifically. As much as I'd love stuck vaults, I know it's not as realistic. So I think all of those, if we hone in on the stuck dismounts, that could be six tenths that I gained back on each event if every girl sticks. So just mathematically I think oh, a potential 1.2 could be added to our score," she said.

On the floor, she was focused on cleaning up leaps and turns. "We've really nailed our tumbling, but we could always do bigger leaps, we could always do prettier dance, showing off our routines. So just kind of cleaning up the little spots.

"I'm very confident in every single girl that I am going to put up in postseason that they can go out there and nail their routine, but right now we just got to really sweat the little details."

Brecksville Bees meet judges at the 2023 state meet. (Courtesy Bill Henning)

Ella Shaheen celebrates with Maria Schneider. (Courtesy Bill Henning)

Above: Alecia Farina competes in the vault event during her senior year. (Courtesy Alecia Farina)

Right: Alecia Farina celebrates her perfect 10. (Courtesy Alecia Farina)

Above left: Lea Haverdill competes on the balance beam. (Courtesy Bill Henning). *Above right:* Kyla Haverdill competes in the floor event. (Courtesy Bill Henning)

Gianna Ravagnani celebrates with Joan Ganim. (Courtesy Bill Henning)

Above left: Ron Ganim was a longtime teacher and coach at Brecksville-Broadview Heights. (Courtesy Maria Schneider). *Above right:* Ron Ganim at Gym World. (Courtesy Maria Schneider)

Ron Ganim with his family. (Courtesy Maria Schneider)

Rachel Kelly and Lea Haverdill embrace after winning the state title. (Courtesy Bill Henning)

Jeanne Winzen competes in the uneven bars at the state competition. (Courtesy Bill Henning)

Rachel Kelly competes in the uneven bars. (Courtesy Bill Henning)

Rachel Kelly hugs Joan Ganim. (Courtesy Bill Henning)

CHAPTER 11

A Fraction of a Point

Though each year Maria, Joan, and Leah thought the Bees could be in danger of losing the state meet, the truth was most recent years they dominated it and won by anywhere between 2 and 8 points. Even in 2022, the year when the gymnasts fell off the beam in their last event and were considerably concerned that they had lost the meet, they ended up winning by more than 2 points.

But in 2000 (before the streak), 2004, 2008, and 2009, the winning score really was only a fraction of a point away from the second-place finisher—and that was what always stuck in Maria's head and something she's passed on to all of her gymnasts. "There's a lot of pressure on us. Especially during practice, you're just thinking about it that's what this is all going to come down to, it could be a tenth of a point and knowing that a bad toe point could lose it all, you need to go through practice with that mindset," she said. "It's really scary."

The meet that was Maria's first experience with a fraction of a point being the difference—and the one she remembered vividly—was the 2000 state meet when Brecksville was neck and neck with rival Magnificat, the team that was the team to beat at the time. The streak hadn't started yet, but Brecksville had already won a state title and had become a strong player in the high school gymnastics world when they found themselves within striking distance of Magnificat going into the final event—floor exercise. Magnificat, after its final event, finished with a 143.975. At the time, Magnificat had won eight of the last ten state meets. Brecksville's Kristen Bohdan led floor exercises with a 9.475 score to secure the win.

From *The Daily Record* newspaper at the time:

> Bohdan, who injured her back during the vault competition to open the day, came back to post a 9.475 in the final floor routine, helping her team edge Magnificat 144–43.975. "This is extra special because we knew it was going to be a tough meet coming in," said Brecksville coach Joan Ganim, who also doubles as assistant for her husband's team, Chardon Notre Dame-Cathedral Latin. "When you have a deep team with six solid gymnasts you hope that when one has a bad routine, the others step up and make up for it. Tonight we did just that."

Eight years later, with the state win streak at five years old, Andrea Kinzer stood over her teammate Diana Moock, watching her as she sat on the ground calculating the scores from other teams across the meet. Diana, a numbers whiz with the nickname "the human calculator," was furiously computing the scores of the competition that the team had gathered through their intel sources. Brecksville had an advantage: The order of events was randomly decided and in their draw that year, they went after Magnificat. But there was bad news: After completing her quick math, Diana looked at the team. "We need to upgrade our skills," she said.

The gymnasts for Brecksville—even in 2008—had a range of skills that they performed for club meets (the harder skills) and often watered them down for high school meets—with the coaches, they would craft routines that were more reliable than the ones they competed with at club meets. But in 2008, the safe routines it seemed, weren't going to get the score they needed. So came plan B on the fly.

Andrea had fractured her right ankle earlier that year and had surgery on her left knee the year before after being injured doing a Yurchenko layout full vault. She changed her vault into an easier one and had planned on competing that at the state meet. But, looking at Diana's scores, she knew it was Yurchenko layout full or bust.

And she wasn't the only one who had to make a last-minute change.

"I remember giving the pep talk in the back and [saying] 'Everyone is upgrading their vaults,'" Andrea said. "Everyone is doing everything. If we don't do that, we are going to lose.'"

"And we knew that. We knew if not every single person in that lineup upgraded their vault, we were going to lose."

Mission agreed upon, the gymnasts got into a line and started their walk out. Ron Ganim grabbed Andrea's shoulder and looked at her with a stern expression. "There is a chance that we may not win this meet today," he told her.

She looked back. "I know," she said.

"Keep your head up high, keep the team focused, keep them going," he responded.

Andrea nodded. She knew. As she led her team out, the thought echoed in her head. "We could lose right now."

A few months earlier, Andrea had decided she was going to quit gymnastics. She had suffered through so many injuries. She was tired of spending forty hours a week in the gym and she had just had enough. "I was done. I was tired. I didn't wanna go to college for it anymore. I was fried, I was exhausted," she remembered.

She told her mom.

"Okay, you are coming home today," her mom told her. "You're not going to practice." And I said, "Okay, I'm not going to practice."

Andrea went home and was sitting at her kitchen table. She watched through the window as a familiar car pulled up, a black SUV. "I was like 'Oh shit,'" she said. Ron, in his signature shorts and polo shirt, came walking up to her door.

"And my mom said, 'Come on in, Mr. G. And I was just like, no, no, no, no, no, don't let him in, don't let him know I'm here. And my mom's like, 'Oh you're here.' My parents were very close with Mr. G too. And he just sat there and looked at me and I just started crying. 'I don't want to do it anymore.'"

Ron sat and listened. "He talked me through it and tried to figure out what was best for me. And at that point I was so over it that he told me, 'Okay, how can we make this better? How can we get you to come back to the gym and find a love for gymnastics again?'"

Andrea didn't know. They came to an agreement. She came into Gym World for a week just by herself and on her terms and worked on what she wanted. It worked. "That helped me get to a place of loving the sport," she remembered.

She eventually resumed her full schedule of training. And as she walked into that gym in 2008, her senior year, the team was depending on her. Magnificat finished with a 147.050. Brecksville trailed by more than 37 points going into the last event, meaning four gymnasts had to average a 9.25 score.

Andrea was the last vaulter up and the team needed a 9.7 or above. She walked up to the start of the vault runway. AJ Ganim, then a Brecksville assistant, stood to the right of the vault, ready to catch her if it went awry, but it wasn't necessary. She landed the first for a 9.7. She heard some taunting in the crowd from other teams. Then she went for her second attempt—and nailed a 9.85. Her teammates, which included Leah Miko, rushed in to congratulate her. There's a video of the moment she'd seen many times since then—one of her favorite moments in it was a shot of Ron Ganim, sitting off to the side of the event. All of a sudden, his hands went up. "And he's all pumping his fist into the air, all that stuff," Andrea said.

Andrea went on to work in an emergency room at a hospital as a nurse. She credited her time on the team with giving her a lot of similar skills as it took to handle her current job. "I'm very good under pressure. I've always been very good under pressure," she said. Even in 2008, when she graduated and the streak was only at five consecutive state titles, she remembered the pressure to win being intense. At the time, busloads of her peers came down to watch the state meet too. "You have not only your parents, you have your coaches, you have your team, and then they also take all these students down on this bus that goes all the way down to Columbus," she said. "And you have your friends and you have the people you're dating and all those people and you just want to do well. And you're young, you're in high school and you're just thinking, oh my God, everyone's eyes are on this team right now. It's easy to crumble, it's easy to hiccup a little bit."

At the time Andrea competed, many of the team's traditions were similar to the 2022–23 team, though the pregame dinners were limited to spaghetti dinners and the poststate meet toilet papering was mostly targeted at the football and hockey team. She loved her relationships with her teammates. "Everyone was very close. And when we were in high school, I don't think we had any other friends besides each other because we're training four hours a day, five days a week. Saturday mornings after going out, after football games, we'd all be there at 6

A.M. or 7 A.M.. Some days, they'd be functioning as a group on five or six hours of sleep each. It was rough.

"That was my second family. I spent more time at the gym than I did at home. I was at school all day and then I'd go to the gym for four hours at night and then I'd get home at eight o'clock, do homework, go to bed. So that was my life. And the Ganims, I always said, well, they're . . . they're my second family. They were always there when I needed it."

She also credited Ron Ganim for being a protector in a sport where—unbeknownst to Andrea and her teammates—when she competed, abuse scandals were festering at the highest levels of gymnastics and the sport was in a crisis that wasn't being openly talked about yet. She remembered going to club meets and camps and being shocked at what she saw.

"I saw these coaches screaming at their gymnast," Andrea remembered. "Mr. Ganim never yelled at me. I would literally laugh if Mr. Ganim yelled at me. He never raised his voice at me. He talked to me like I was an equal." The memories of the other coaches still stuck with her. "I saw [one coach] scream at a girl and call her all sorts of names because she fell on a floor routine. And then seeing a couple others [from other gyms] cursing at their gymnasts on the vault."

She remembered Ron calmly guiding them away from scenes like that. "We're going over here," he would tell them. "We're not a part of this."

Ron was strict about keeping the Gym World gymnasts away from other teams—something that frustrated Andrea at the time, but she later understood.

"They're all going out, they're all doing things. And he said, 'No, curfew's nine o'clock tape's going on your door. If I see that tape broken on your door, you're gonna be in trouble.'"

The Gym World gymnasts would instead stay in their room, watch TV, play board games and just hang out together before turning out the lights."

It was the first thing Andrea thought about when she started to read the news stories about allegations against high ranking USA Gymnastics coaches, officials, and medical staff as the proverbial dam broke in 2016 starting with an *Indianapolis Star* newspaper story that reported USA Gymnastics took complaints about abuse by coaches and filed them away without taking action.

Andrea read the stories of the US Olympic gymnasts accusing USA Gymnastics in lawsuits of failing to protect gymnasts from sexual abuse by the team doctor. She read the stories of the gymnasts who filed complaints with the FBI, USA Gymnastics officials, and other coaches for years only to be ignored. And she read the stories of the testimony from the gymnasts who testified against Nassar, the team doctor, and told the stories of terror they experienced at his hands while they were trying to live their dreams of competing at the highest level.

And with each news story, she immediately thought of the contrast to her experience and thought of it often as the news stories continued to come.

After her Gym World and Brecksville-Broadview Heights High School career, Andrea went on to compete for Bowling Green—Leah Miko was her teammate there as well—but for her, she said, the highlight of her career was being coached by the Ganims and contributing to four high school state titles. She thought often, knowing the world of gymnastics she was competing in and adjacent to, how different it could have been.

"I thought, thank God, thank you so much," she said. Ron Ganim, "kept us protected."

Now married and living again in the Cleveland area, Andrea ran into people who remembered who she was in Ohio high school gymnastics. At work, she remembered one of the new physicians came in and looked on the nurses' board—and stopped. "She asked, 'Were you Andrea Kinzer, the gymnast?'" Andrea said. "I said, 'Yup, that was me.' She told me, 'I followed you all through high school. It was amazing.'"

And the Brecksville-Broadview Heights High School team that she competed with, she said, still had a close bond. A few years ago, the father of one of her teammates passed away. "Every one of us showed up," she said. "Her mom made a post and said, 'You know, it's crazy to see the amount of people that we haven't seen in years.' I mean, I haven't been in high school in 10, 15 years and she was [amazed by] the amount of people we haven't seen who showed up for this funeral."

The reason they were all there, of course, was simple.

"Because that was your family," Andrea said. "You might not talk to them forever, but that's still family."

The 2009 state meet was even closer—Andrea had graduated and was in her freshman year at Bowling Green. But Leah was still on the team and the Bees beat Magnificat by .125. According to the recap from the *Cleveland Plain Dealer,* Brecksville overcame "its worst performance of the season on the balance beam and became the first school in Ohio to win six consecutive gymnastic championships."

The Bees had to recover from the beam event with their "best performance of the season on the uneven bars, the last event of the day." The Bees scored a meet-high 36.700 on the uneven bars—.075 higher than Magnificat in that event.

Despite Maria's concerns, going into the 2023 state meet, no one has come within a point of beating them since.

CHAPTER 12

Postseason Arrives

As the regular season came to an end, Rachel's top skills still hadn't returned. She was working with her club coaches at the practices she did with them during the week to rebuild them, a process that included starting back at square one for a skill and building it back up to a point where she was confident and ready to compete it. But progress was slow going and one day at a high school practice, Rachel's frustration boiled over.

She finished her practice and was getting ready to go home when she saw Ella talking to Leah and Maria. The seniors' practice had finished a few minutes earlier. Ella left their high school coaches and walked over to Rachel.

The coaches were at a loss about what to do. Ella, a team captain, had been in similar situations before. Maybe, they hoped, she could figure out what Rachel needed.

"Can I talk to you for a second?" she asked.

"Yeah," Rachel replied, the practice and season's frustration still stinging.

The two went to the empty conditioning room above the gym floor to talk privately.

They sat down. Ella looked at Rachel. "We need to figure out whatever's going on," she said. "We need you," she added.

She asked what she could do to help.

Rachel knew what she was saying. It was about to be postseason. She was part of the team score, an important score in all four events. And somewhere in there, she knew she could do it. She just didn't know how. She was so frustrated that she had firmly shut herself off from her teammates. She just wanted to be left alone. She wasn't mad at Ella—she was grateful for the senior captain's support. But she was done hearing it from her other teammates.

"I'm just done with everybody coming up to me and saying, 'You need to figure this out,'" Rachel said. "Like it was just me, that I needed to do this so that the team wouldn't be hurt. I had to do this, I had to do that."

It was making her feel the pressure, which was already growing to be too much, even worse. So that's what she told Ella.

"I just need people to stop coming up to me and saying it's up to me to do this and it's up to me to do that," she told Ella.

Ella understood. They just needed to let her work through this.

The two sat and wrote in Rachel's Psychobabble journal some small goals to accomplish each practice. She just had to keep building enough to run through that block.

. . .

As Rachel was trying to get over her mental blocks, the Brecksville parents were busy getting ready for everything they needed to do for the state meet even though they technically hadn't qualified yet. "It's time to start thinking about states and what we can do to celebrate our girls and help get them pumped for the meet!" one parent wrote in the group chat. "We are their biggest fans and every year the parents make states week special for them with gift bags, bus decorations and a fun send off as they get on the bus to travel to the meet in Columbus. GIFT BAGS: A gift will be purchased for each girl from the team fund and Melissa and I are coordinating the bags they will receive on the bus. Donations are welcome to add to their bags! To give you an idea of what has been done in the past, families donate special snacks for them to have throughout the weekend like cake pops, chocolate covered Oreos, snack mixes etc. Last year they also received things like Pure Vida bracelets, keychains, string backpacks, Bees winter hats, a Bee necklace, Bees blankets and fuzzy socks. This is totally optional! Jocelyn, Christi & Melissa have generously donated engraved bracelets this year. Let's post here if you would like to make a donation so we don't duplicate each other. BUS SENDOFF: The bus leaves from Gym World the morning of the state meet—Please plan on joining us that morning if you can! The parents gather in the parking lot to decorate the bus and see the girls off. Last year we had a break thru banner that the girls ran through and we released confetti poppers and had music playing outside of the gym. They have a police escort with a parent caravan of cars to the highways so it's a lot of fun for them. Jessica and I are coordinating the send off. We are not allowed to release balloons so please let us know if you have any fun ideas!"

The ideas quickly flowed in. A candy bag of Bees-themed candy. Red socks with bees on them. Personalized Starbucks tumblers. Festive Rice Krispies treats. "I have 18 bee cutouts, 2 different sizes, if anyone wants these for decorating anything," Delaney's mom offered. A pouch embroidered with "Bee Happy" with Chapstick and glitter eyeliners inside. "I have a personalized bee ornament and some full candy treats," another mom offered.

Leah weighed in: "I know their theme is 'just rock' this year so maybe something for the walk out relating to that [rockstar-like I'm assuming] lol," she wrote.

"I got pop rocks and rock candy and I'm going to try to make 'let's rock' labels if I have time," Janelle Henning wrote.

"I can already hear the popping on the bus," Kim responded. "They'll love them!!"

Meanwhile, Rachel's mom Jessica was organizing a team dinner at Wild Eagle, a large restaurant/bar with arcade games right off the highway exit to Broadview Heights. She used her connections to organize a night before the Conference Championship, the first official postseason meet, a night to have fun and relax for the team and their families. In an email, she sent out a spreadsheet to gauge what she should have ready.

"The Wild Eagle has donated the food, soft drinks and games for the team only, I understand there is a nut allergy and will ensure that is accommodated. We will stack the jukebox with a combination of dance music and country. We will have the space next to the games. Families and Coaches are welcome and encouraged to join, we will have a great time!! Again, the team is taken care of, the rest of us are on our own—they just want to know how many plan to eat meals, or we could just order apps for the table.

"Please take a few minutes to complete the attached spreadsheet so we know how many will be joining us.

"See you all then!!!"

The Conference Championship was mostly a dry run for the post-season meets that counted to state meet: sectionals and districts. The Bees competed in the Suburban League, made up of Hudson, Highland, Twinsburg, Wadsworth, Stow, Aurora, Nordonia, North Royalton, and Revere High School. Of those schools, only Hudson participated in the state meet the year before. Highland's lineup included gymnast Paige Yu, a senior who had won the individual all-around, uneven bars, and balance beam as a sophomore in the 2021 state meet. Before the start of the next season, she dislocated her knee landing a vault in a club meet and missed the high school season. With her return this year, she was expected again to place highly, if not win the state meet individual all-around even if it was unlikely for her to take her team with her to Columbus.

Despite the relatively low stakes of the meet, it was the biggest pre-meet dinner that the team had had yet. Jessica wanted to celebrate the gymnasts starting postseason and make sure the gymnasts knew how proud they were of them. On the night of the dinner, the parents sat at tables in a room toward the back of the restaurant, talking quietly over appetizers and a few beers. In the room next to them were the gymnasts, picking at pizza, mozzarella sticks, and other options from a buffet table and sitting in groups on the couch. Lea, Rachel, Kyla, and a few other girls gathered on one of the couches eating together. Lea and Rachel had already started going through their premeet rituals, which included writing their "angel numbers" on their ankles, a type of numerology calculated according to birthdays. The dinner at Wild Eagle was also likely their last solid meal before the meet. "I can't eat before," Lea said. "Maybe tomorrow I'll eat something light in the morning, but I can't eat before."

Rachel, on the other hand, loaded up on candy. "I always do good when I eat bad, but I eat good and I do bad in the meet," she explained.

In the room where most of the parents had been relegated, Todd Haverdill had split concerns: The wrestling team faced perennial powerhouse St. Edward's the next day in the Division 1 state dual tournament championship, a tournament that St. Edward's hadn't lost since 2019. "I've got my own things to worry about," he said, sighing.

The girls eventually divided into games across the restaurant. Lea and Rachel sat in a driving game, the King Kong of Skull Island VR Arcade Game, where participants "explore the mysteries and dangers that lurk across Skull Island through three immersive episodes," giggling hysterically and yelling. Todd came over and saw the two of them wearing the VR headsets and tried to mess with his daughter, who was crouched with her hands above her head, swatting off real (her dad) and fake (the game) interferences. "Lea," Rachel shouted as she put her hands in front of her VR headset trying to grab at something. "Where are you going?"

On the other side of the bar, a number of gymnasts put on gold, red, or black hats (Bees' colors) and Ella led a game of bags, patiently explaining the rules to anyone who hadn't played before and trying to fairly judge who was over the allowed line. Delaney looked over at her team. The next day was the first time that they would be doing what was expected to be their "real lineups," or at least, in current form, the ones most likely to be the lineups at states. "I think everyone's excited to see how we're doing," she said.

There was also a punching bag game that the gymnasts lined up to try. It was good, Rachel said, for them to get out their anger and anxiety.

Rachel's grandmother Stephanie sat on the couch watching the gymnasts giggle and enjoy themselves. Earlier that day, she had chatted with Rachel about the upcoming few weeks and her lingering mental blocks and self-doubt. "I said, 'You're the it girl,'" she said. "You got it. When you get up there, you just say to yourself, 'I got it. I'm the it girl.' She just kind of looked at me. I said, 'You girls have what other people don't. You have it.' I said, 'Have you ever heard of the it factor?' And she looked at me and then I explained to her what the factor was. I said, 'So now you can tell yourself *I got it.* So let's see if it works.'"

. . .

Four hours before the meet, Delaney's mom Jennifer took to the group chat. "Hey parents, it's time to Just Rock!!" she wrote. "Let's start the post season off today with a BLACK OUT. Mark and I will arrive early and save seats in the center section so we can sit together. And we are looking for a cheerleader to start off our chants! 'B! E!"

Maria replied: "E! S!"

. . .

From the moment she woke up the day of the Conference Championships, Bailey knew something was off. "I was already having a rough morning," she said later. "I wasn't in the right mindset."

Her warm-up, she would say later, was off. "I think I only flipped one vault."

She was the first competitor in the first event, vault, for Brecksville. It was her chance to continue to solidify her spot in vault as a freshman at the state meet. It was her first postseason meet of her high school career.

"And then I just remember before my vault, I wasn't even thinking about the vault," she said later.

She wasn't mentally prepared. She was just worried. The stress started to creep in. "I have to do this," she told herself.

She wasn't thinking about herself, she was thinking about her coaches.

She was just in her head.

She ran up.

But her technique was off.

"I opened up too early," she said.

She landed short and crumpled to the ground. Leah and a trainer rushed over.

Bailey knew instantly.

"This isn't good," she thought.

She looked at Leah as tears filled her eyes. "I'm sorry," she told her. Leah assured her it was okay. Bailey started to cry more. "I just felt awful," she said later. "I felt like I let the team down."

Kyla, Brooke, and her other teammates rushed over to comfort her.

She was helped into a side room by the trainer, who examined her and said her injury wasn't rush-to-the-hospital serious. She could stay at the meet and get it looked at later. Lexi, one of the Padua gymnasts, had come to cheer on the team at the meet and sat next to Bailey as the two of them watched from a spot right outside of the equipment room on the side of the gym.

As Bailey composed herself and sat watching from the side with her leg elevated, she started doing math. Sectionals was in a week. Districts two. States three. She'd do physical therapy intensively, she thought, and make it back in time for districts at least.

"I have to push through," she thought.

Somehow, Ella had to follow her on the vault. She scored a 9. Emily went third and earned a 9.5, a huge moment that uplifted the team from the shock of Bailey's injury. Emily had upgraded her vault to a Yurchenko layout, one that would earn her .5 points more than the vault she had been competing all season. It was a huge addition to the team score.

And then Rachel went up.

She looked at the vault.

Earlier that week at a club practice, Rachel decided that she had had enough with her mental block. "We're going to lose if I don't get this together," she thought.

So she just went into practice and made a decision. "You know what, we're just going to do it," she told herself. "We're going to see how it goes. If I die, I die. But at least I tried."

It worked. She completed her high school competition vault.

But that was just practice.

This was a meet.

In an effort to stop Rachel from psyching herself out in warm-ups, Leah came up with a plan earlier in the season. Rachel did one vault and then no more. When it was time to compete, she wouldn't even warm up.

So at this meet, that's what Rachel did. But even her single warm-up vault was bad. She awkwardly shot forward and landed weirdly. She walked away. Not a great omen. And, to make matters worse for her already-anxious brain, there was Bailey's injury.

When it was her turn to compete, Rachel ran down to the vault. "Now or never," she thought. She tried to erase her mind as she launched into a handspring front tuck vault, the one that she was going to compete at state. She stuck her landing and turned to the judges, hands up and with a huge surprised smile on her face.

Her team exploded. Rachel felt herself hyperventilating. She had done it. Leah ran in with her arms up in excitement. She wrapped her in a huge hug. Maria ran down the vault to congratulate her. Finally.

"Do you want do it again?" Leah asked.

Rachel laughed.

Absolutely not.

"I'm done," she said. "I'm walking away."

Leah thought it was the best vault she had seen in her coaching career.

They turned and waited for the judge.

9.35.

"Robbed," Rachel thought. Leah pretended to slam an iPad on her knee in frustration. Maria was livid. "The same vault went two tenths higher than Rachel's," she said later, still mad.

"I was going to challenge it," Maria said later. "But I talked to the judge and she wasn't going to change it."

It didn't really matter. If it was state meet, of course, it would have been a different story. Maria would have challenged it.

After the meet, Leah posted a clip of the vault on the team's Instagram account.

"Make. It. Count," she wrote. "#bees #gymnastics #postseason #lfg #makeitcount"

Rachel was back.

And just in time.

And she wanted Starburst.

The year before, Leah asked the gymnasts what she should do for them if they made it through a beam routine without falls. Even before the state meet, beam had been a point of frustration for her all year and she had expected answers like less conditioning or something. Instead, the gymnasts had a singular demand: Candy.

It was something that remained on the table for everything in this season. The night before conference meet, Leah had had a weird feeling. A good weird feeling. She ordered a few packages of Starburst, Rachel's favorite, just in case. "I paid extra for last-minute delivery," she said. But she didn't tell anyone. As soon as Rachel hit her vault, she knew what Leah had to hand over as part of the ongoing deal. "I don't have them," Leah replied, fibbing. "I'll have to get it for you next time."

At the end of the meet, she threw the candy in Rachel's bag.

Following her, GG came in with a 9.6. Brooke, a freshman, finished the lineup with 7.9. It wasn't a surprising low score—she had just done a handspring. She had been hurt all season, and the coaches had wanted to give her a chance to compete. "Ms. Schneider thought I deserved to compete one time at one meet, which was really nice of her," Brooke said. Even though she was mostly healed from her ankle injury suffered in gym class, her knees were still giving her trouble. "When I did gymnastics a few years ago, I had really bad knee problems and that's one of the reasons I quit too. But my knee problems were coming back from the high school gymnastics team, but I decided just to power through it because I really wanted to compete," she said.

Leah was left with two questions in the vault and one answer—Rachel was back. GG was as solid as she was last year. Ella, a senior, would be fine. Emily, the freshman, would be a much-needed addition. They were the only school in the state, Leah thought, with three vaults with a 10.0 start value. But the last two spots were in question—and as a team, they only had five flipping vaults.

Next came bars. The lineup was Emily, Rachel, Lea, Ella, Jeanne, and GG. Ella, who came in second on uneven bars in the state meet her sophomore year, put up an impressive 9.35, earning an excited dance from Leah. When it came to GG's turn, there was a hiccup. She slipped off the bar. She shook her head and adjusted her wrist guard. "It's alright," her teammates shouted. "You got this, GG!"

She walked over to get more hand chalk.

Leah crouched down to talk to her.

She got up and competed again. Just as Leah had been hoping—this season she had said she was coaching her girls to fight through mistakes instead of letting them give up on it.

Next came beam, which was shakier—a warning of a repeat of the 2022 disaster on beam. Out of the six competitors—Lea, GG, Ella, Jeanne, Emily, and Rachel—only GG scored over 9.1.

Floor exercise gave Leah another reason to hope. Rachel hadn't figured out her mental block, but she had played around enough with her routine that she swapped in a new pass with skills she was comfortable with that were equivalent in score to the one that had been tripping her up. Ella and Delaney had also added an important element into their floor routines. At one point in each, they did moves to show putting a crown on their heads to signify that as seniors, they were the Queen Bees.

The Bees won the conference championship easily with a team score of 145.6, more than 5 points higher than Hudson in the second spot. Paige Yu won the all-around with a 37.45. GG came in third in the all-around at 36.7. Ella came in second on uneven bars .3 points behind Paige's. Ella finished fourth in floor and all-around. Emily took second on vault, Jeanne fourth on uneven bars.

It was a good start to the postseason.

But something had frustrated them.

Rachel looked out during her beam routine and saw some familiar faces—faces who weren't competing in the meet or who they thought were there to cheer on friends. The top six gymnasts in rival school Brunswick's rotation.

It wasn't unusual for other teams to show up to watch their friends' routines or check out the competition and see the difficulty level of their skills. Brecksville gymnasts, in fact, had been doing it all season. Some of the Brecksville gymnasts had gone to two of Brunswick's meets and one of Medina's to check out the competition—more than they had done in previous years. "It's closer this year," Lea explained. "Other years we were winning by a couple of points. And those two teams are our biggest competition so it feels better going into the meet knowing what they can do."

But to the Brecksville gymnasts, this felt different, with the Brunswick gymnasts sitting noticeably in the stands. They weren't friendly with them. It felt pointed the way that they were sitting there watching and cheering for other teams. No one could explain exactly why. It just bugged them.

"I think it did get in their head yesterday," Leah said the next day. "You know, beam is definitely not our strongest event. It's our weakest. And it kind of got to them. I only have three upperclassmen in the beam lineup and then three underclassmen and even my upperclassmen don't have much experience aside from Ella in the beam lineup."

The Bees knew that people disliked them. No one liked eternal winners. They felt like no one clapped for them when they won or were excited for game-changing moments they have provided year after year. But they knew they could never respond with anything negative to other teams. "I think the biggest thing that myself and Maria instill in the girls is to be a good sport," Leah said. "Anytime that there's an away meet, we are always helping [to] clean up. Just because we know what it's like. We host a lot of meets and we just don't ever see that reciprocated from many teams. So I just try to teach them to always be the bigger person. As easy as it is to fall into social media and you know, post about this person or post about this team, we don't do it. And I know, I'm guilty of it too. My first couple years of coaching, I wanted to have that competitive side, but it just adds so much extra drama and stress that we don't need."

They had bigger things to focus on, though.

The next day they gathered for a walk-through of a practice, wearing T-shirts and shorts instead of their leos. They worked on fine-tuning the little things—the things that provided or deducted tenths of points that they wanted back. "I think yesterday's meet lit a fire underneath the girls' butts because I think they realized we have a lot of work to do and it's not going to come easy," Leah said. "But I think it's better now that this is happening now than a month ago, because they would have started to be burned out by now. I saw a different side of the girls come together after the meet and even today at practice and to just see how much they really do want this, which I know me and Maria haven't really seen all season."

There was also another big wake-up call that came. A 145.6 might have been good enough to win a conference championship, which was a nice thing to have.

But in Columbus, the Berlin Olentangy team had competed in their conference championship as well.

"Bears Gymnastics takes 1ST IN THE OCC for the 4TH YEAR IN A ROW, breaking the previous SCHOOL RECORD again with a 146.725," they reported on their Twitter account. "#roadtostates23 #lightthis-candle #clawsup @Todd_spinner @BerlinBearsAD @BerlinStrength."

It was a lot of hashtags. None of them were related to the Bees. But unintentionally or not, the tweet—and more importantly, the result—seemed to Leah and Maria to be a warning shot directly at them.

CHAPTER 13

Sectionals

Jeanne's club coach, Jess Kaiser, had good news for Maria in the days leading up to sectionals. Jeanne upgraded some of her skills on uneven bars and they could be ready in time for competition. It happened during the garbage time of practice. She had her bar routine down easily—it was a cast handstand pirouette, clear hip, giants on the high bar to layout. "I'd just hit it every single time, so then I would get done with the routines we had to do for practice and then we would just mess around with other little things," Jeanne said.

She realized that some of the more difficult skills were coming to her consistently in an upgraded routine of a clear hip squat on, giant blind front, giant pirouette, and then layout.

Her club coaches noticed too. "Do you want to compete those?" they asked.

Jeanne was taken aback.

It was her first year that she was able to compete at the state meet—and postseason was already here. She had had a career littered with injuries and had started off the season with a bad mental block of her own. It wasn't as bad as Rachel's, but it lasted for a few days. "I was convinced I would peel off the bar so I wouldn't do my second half of my bar routine," she said. "I would jump down because I was scared I was going to fly off the bar. And so then one time I convinced myself to do it and I did fly off the bar so that made it worse." Luckily, it lasted only one meet and then she got her confidence back. Changing a routine not only meant that she was more likely to make a mistake, but also that she could mentally have a block.

It seemed risky to change a solid routine.

But it would also help the team, which needed every tenth of a point it could get—it could be an additional two or three tenths of a point. Her teammates—her club practices included Rachel, Ella, Bailey, Delaney, Avery, and GG—noticed too. Eventually Rachel stood beside the uneven bars as Jeanne practiced yelling. "If you do this, we're winning states," she would shout, alternating often with "Don't you dare fall!"

So she decided she would try it—at least at sectionals, the first round of the postseason that mattered. All she had to do was finish in the top twelve in the event to advance to districts as an individual and Brecksville had to finish as a team in the top four. There was room for her to drop a few (or more) tenths of points on mistakes if she could get to a place to compete the upgraded routine at the district and state meet.

The Bees' parents were also getting ready. "It's postseason and time to ROCK our team spirit!" Delaney's mom Jennifer posted to the group. "Let's form a unified cheering section and GET LOUD this Saturday! Jessica will be saving seats. Here are our colors for our next meets: Sectionals 2/18—WHITE. Districts 2/25—RED. States 3/3—BLACK."

They also were planning a potluck lunch for the team and trying to coordinate lunch for districts to be a step ahead. And Tish, Sara's mom, was planning ahead to the state meet already. Her responsibility was for the poststate meet dinner that the team held at the hotel. The night after the team day at the state meet, the team had a late dinner at the hotel together as a celebration. "I think I need some help," she wrote in the group chat. "I signed up to get the cake for states. I have researched places in Hilliard to get the cake, there are not a lot. This has to be a full size cake, correct? Not cupcakes? Does it matter? To further complicate this, there is a slight chance we (parents) are not going to be able to go to the state meet now. If there is anyone who wanted to take on getting the cake, I would be happy to switch for another responsibility or I could still order and pay for the cake if someone else could pick up if we are not able to go to the meet."

Avery's mom chimed in. She had been in charge of the cake last year and had picked it up in Columbus. "The more complicated part," she wrote, "was what to do with the cake. I think we picked it up before we headed to the state meet and kept it in the car because it was cold outside. We weren't sure the hotel would take it and after the meet was too late. It worked out but another thing to consider!"

. . .

But first came sectionals, which was held at Hudson High School, a school thirty minutes southeast of Brecksville. The Bees were scheduled to compete on bars first. Jeanne warmed up her new routine in the back auxiliary gym. She hit it once—a good sign—so decided to go with it in the meet. Warming up on the competition bars a few minutes later, though, her hand slipped. She tried again—same thing. Feelings of anxiety and fear starting welling up. Looking on and watching the whole thing unfold, Leah made a quick choice. "It's okay," she told Jeanne. "Just do your old routine here and you'll compete your new one at districts." Jeanne nodded, relieved.

Emily kicked off the bars, then Rachel and Lea. Jeanne had the fourth spot and performed her old routine for a serviceable 9.0 score. Ella, hoping to repeat as a top performer on bars at state meet, went fifth and came in with a 9.1. GG was the anchor. Leah could tell something was wrong even before she started. GG's confidence had drained. She had hit so many in the back gym, which was perfect and she had had a good one in warm-up, so Leah hadn't been too nervous. But in competition, GG's hand slipped and she fell for the second time in two weeks. Her score, an 8.575, meant that she wouldn't advance as an individual to compete bars in the state meet.

"I think she just got in her own head a little bit and she thought about conference where she fell and I think that just carries with any gymnast from the last meet to the next meet, especially with so much pressure riding on this one," Leah said. "Unfortunately, she didn't qualify out on bars, which sucks because she could be in the top six on bars in the state, but I think it's definitely giving her some motivation for this upcoming week to hit that routine."

It was a shakier outcome than the team had hoped for going into beam.

At the start of the season, Leah had been working to get the gymnasts in a better mental state for beam. Leah and Maria had them do visualizations and say personal affirmations as they walked up to salute the judges. But at the conference championship the week before, it hadn't been working as well as she had wanted. So for sectionals, it was time to try something different.

For warm-ups, they lined up and imitated so-called "model walks"—silly, exaggerated glamorous strolls down the beam/runway set to music to get them loose. Then Ella gathered the five other gymnasts competing in beam—Lea, GG, Emily, Avery, and Rachel in the auxiliary gym. They knelt in a circle, eyes closed, and Ella recited a meditation that she had learned from a coach to help her beam routine earlier in her career. "Close your eyes," she said. "Think of the time slowing down and we have time for everything in the world right now. Things that we want to do and things that you know we have to do. Picture yourself at a relaxing place like the beach and think of just feeling the air around you and the wind. Think that you're at the beach. And then also think of a place in your body that could be a relaxation point and just think of that place when you want to be relaxed and it'll bring you into a relaxing state."

Then they went into breathing exercises.

Leah had also made another tactical change: The gymnasts weren't going to watch the ones who went before them. "That way they're not in the environment of the girl that's competing," she explained. "That way they have no idea what's going on. I think if girls watch their teammate before, as good as it can be, if one person hits and you see that, you think okay, now I can go up and hit my routine too. It builds a positive momentum in that sense. But we've also seen the downfall of that too, even if I have two girls in a row that stick, their beam routine, that third one still will put self-induced pressure on themselves. And then it turned negative." So she was trying a new method for sectionals—"to just remove them from the situation so they don't know if the routine before was good or if it was bad," she said. "They're not in the gym and it's already loud as it is so they can't differentiate if the clapping was for the girl on beam or the girl on floor."

So in the gym, the rest of the team took their usual spots on the side of the beam to cheer. But GG, Ella, Emily, Avery, and Rachel sat in the back gym, unable to see what happened as Lea went up first for beam. 8.875.

Then it was up to GG. The year before in the state meet, GG had fallen twice on beam. She had worked hard ever since to rebuild her confidence in the event and become a dependable competitor in it for the Bees. Especially after her uncharacteristic fall in bars, the coaches were watching closely to see if she could mentally keep it together. She scored a 9.25.

Ella came out and looked at the stands. Her parents had unfurled a huge fathead poster of her. She was mortified and sent a message through Maria: "She wants to know if you could kindly put the fathead away," Maria said. Her parents laughed and followed instructions. She scored an 8.9125, then Emily with an 8.8. Avery, the sophomore, hit a 9.050 and Rachel finished with a 9.025. Much better than at the conference meet.

The team had made a lot of adjustments since that meet too—in addition to the prebeam routine. They decided to redo the order to start with the gymnast most dependable to hit her routine. "And we determined Lea, she's hit 100 percent of the season so far and when she hits, she goes 8.85, 8.9, which is exactly where we want to start and then keep building from there," Leah said. "We put GG second because even though she's our best beam worker, she also, the later she waits, the more in her head she gets, so get her out of the way. So then she went 9.25 and Ella is the same way. Ella's rhythm is a little bit better than GG, so that's why she went afterwards. And then after that we have Emily, so she's our freshman. We did have her last because she has the most difficulty in her beam routine, but as a freshman going last on beam is just a lot of pressure that she just wasn't ready for. So we put her fourth this week and she actually hit her most beautiful beam routine. Still needs room for work, but we added a switch loop into hers as well. And then we put Avery. Avery hasn't been in the beam lineup at all. We put her in there. She ended up qualifying out for districts with a 9.05."

That change meant Jeanne hadn't competed in the beam, as she had the week before, but she was still on the lineup for floor and bars. The coaches had told Avery the day before the meet that she would be in the lineup and were pleasantly surprised with her best performance yet—and with an upgraded routine. "And then we ended on Rachel just because she's honestly a hit or miss. So if she hits, she's our strongest beam worker, but if she misses and she's up in the lineup, then that definitely screws with the rest of the girls in the lineup."

Her beam routine, though, while scored lower than the coaches thought she deserved, was more than solid.

After beam, the team gathered around Joan, Leah, and Maria. They congratulated them on a good beam performance and told them it was time to focus on the next event: floor. Then, Joan got a big smile on her face as she broke out into a song: The Black Eyed Peas' 'I Gotta Feeling' with a bit of an adaptation. "Tonight's going to be a good good day," she sang as the group danced and clapped along. The hardest event was over.

Next up came the floor exercise, one of the Bees' stronger events. Delaney was especially nervous. She had put herself, she thought, in a good place to be in the state meet lineup for floor exercise.

She watched as Emily went first, putting up a 9.125 score. Then she went up with a good start to her routine. She had caught the energy of the meet, but then, in a pass, she fell. Her face fell and she quickly tried to recover, but in her head, the damage was done. She ended the routine by mimicking putting a crown on her head, the new tradition. Her team gathered to wave their arms. All hail the queen. But her heart wasn't in it by then.

Delaney felt like anything but the Queen Bee. Her score came in at an 8.050. She was devastated. She was worried she was going to lose her spot in the state lineup.

But to the coaches, it was just a bad meet. "One mistake isn't going to keep you from the state lineup," they told her. "You earned a spot."

Jeanne earned a 9.175; Ella a 9.25 (and a similar crown on her head); Rachel, confident with her new passes on her floor routine, earned a 9.3; and GG came in with a 9.225. Two weeks after not being able to do two of four of her events, Rachel was in line with GG in the all-around competition. Everything was coming together—at least for her.

The last event was vault. Bailey had been going to physical therapy every day, but was still sidelined. Lea kicked off the event, earning an 8.3. Then came Abby, the junior who was battling for a spot in the state lineup in vault. She had a valuable vault when she hit it, but it was inconsistent, leaving the coaches unsure if they could trust her in the lineup. Her warm-ups weren't encouraging. She couldn't land one. She lined up for her first of two attempts. A miss.

Leah started to walk down with her. "Abby," she said. "This vault is only six seconds long. So I need you to go 150 percent."

Abby nodded.

"Be tight, be aggressive, and know you're going to make it."

"Okay," Abby replied. "I got it."

Abby started to run. "She's got it," Leah thought.

Abby did her vault and stuck the landing. She looked to the judges' table. When she saw a 9.1, she covered her mouth in shock.

Two years earlier in sectionals, when Abby was a freshman, doctors thought she fractured her leg on a vault. She had spent the next two years trying to get back to a competitive spot mentally and physically. What Leah realized was the less they do at practice, the better they performed at a meet. "I think the more reps she does, she starts to get in her own head and back to old habits," Leah said later, so she had been limiting the number of vaults.Abby did—she hadn't even vaulted until the day before the meet.

Ella followed with a 9.225, then Emily with another 9.5. Next came Rachel. There were still some rules in place to keep Rachel from getting mentally blocked on her vault. Mainly, according to her mom Jessica, no cheering, so the parents and gymnasts waited quietly as Rachel lined up. She nailed it. A 9.55. GG came next, earning a 9.65.

GG, Rachel, Emily, and Ella qualified for the individual competition for district and in vault, bars, and floor. GG and Avery qualified for the individual competition for beam.

Leah thought it was a huge meet for Rachel especially, and one that she hoped she would take to heart after her finish as the highest Bee in the all-around score (she finished behind Highland's Paige Yu and Tessa, the Padua gymnast who was trained with Brecksville). "[Rachel] Kelly works hard and she can be neck and neck with GG, who's this all-star and talked about in the newspapers and, you know, record books and different things like that," Leah said. In that meet, Leah thought, Rachel finally realized she could be that good too.

The team easily won the meet. "#justrock #LFG #makeitcount #letseat ," Leah wrote on Instagram. They finished with a 147, the highest this year. The next day, Brunswick and Medina would finish their sectionals with scores of 146.25—far too close for comfort—but scores that were below the Bees.

Postseason meet number one down. They had two weeks to go in the season. Next came districts and then state.

CHAPTER 14

"Sickness Is a Mindset"

With five days to go before districts and twelve before the state meet, Maria and Leah got some bad news before practice.

Three of the gymnasts were throwing up.

"If your daughter is not feeling well, please don't send to practice," Maria messaged the parents. "I wonder how this virus is going to spread. Hopefully not at all! Not ever going to enforce a mask but if they want to wear one obviously they can. If stomach hurts stay home! We need practice but we need a healthy team more importantly. GO BEES!"

By the time she finished sending that message, another Bee was down. "Up to 4," she wrote. "Please check on your kiddos. Practice is going to end at 10 also since low numbers and we don't want to up any more risk. Thank you for understanding."

"Hand washing and Purell! That's the best defense against these gastrointestinal infections, like Norovirus," Delaney's dad responded.

Veronica, Kyla, GG, and Tessa Long were the four sick at home.

The culprit was unknown. There were theories floating. The day before, Kyla, GG, Ella, Rachel, Lea, and Bailey had gone as a group to watch the second day of the sectional meet. They wanted to cheer on some of their friends on other teams and check out the competition. They all went out to eat after the meet. A few hours later, Kyla realized something was wrong. She didn't feel good. Then she vomited. "Oh no," she thought immediately. "Not now. It's district's week." After she threw up for the second time, her phone buzzed. "Are you feeling okay?" GG asked. A few minutes after sending that text, GG had started vomiting too. They were both up throughout the night throwing up—for Kyla, a total of nine times.

Maria stood next to the balance beam and watched as Lea, Kyla's sister, sat treacherously close to her teammates. She immediately thought of Kyla's illness and wondered if Lea was spreading whatever bug it was to the rest of the Bees. "Get away from everyone," Maria said aloud, but not loud enough for Lea to hear. "I guess if it happens now, at least everyone will get over it in time."

Maria couldn't remember a time when such a large number of gymnasts had been sick this close to state meet. "Well, Erin [Delahunty], remember Erin was super sick at sectionals. The beginning of COVID," Leah said, pointing back to the postseason days before everything was shut down for the COVID-19 pandemic in 2020.

"And then we had one girl, during the state championship, she puked in the middle of floor," Maria said.

Joan and Maria had also kept close tabs on the second day of the sectional meet—Leah would have too, but she was bartending at her third (or fourth, depending on how you counted it) job, though the gymnasts texted her all of the relevant information in real time. Brecksville's scores were higher, but it did not calm the coaches' nerves. "After two rotations yesterday, there were three teams ahead of us," Maria said. "I know that it all comes back at the end, but we have to hit to be consistent. But it made me feel better that I know we can do it. 147 was our goal. So we hit our goal and then hopefully we can continue that and go up."

Berlin was also scheduled to compete Saturday at their district meet. "This girl from Berlin, the freshman, went 38.3 or something all-around. She's good," Maria reported.

Maria looked over at Ella, who had added a switch leap switch to her beam routine. "Just don't drop your shoulder to the left," she warned.

Avery also upgraded her series to add another few extra tenths of a point. And Rachel upgraded her floor routine to include something backwards—an important element that was missing in the sectional meet. The floor judges didn't catch it, but the overall meet referee did and the coaches didn't want to risk that going into districts and states. "It's a half of a tenth of a point," Maria said. "We threw in just a back tuck somewhere."

At the end of practice, the gymnasts went up to the second floor of the gym for stretching and started discussing the sudden onset of vomit that had overtaken their teammates. "It's food poisoning," Rachel said. "I'm calling it."

They were worried. What if they were all throwing up with only days to go before the district meet? Even though they could easily finish in the top six to make the state meet as a team, getting to day two as individual competitors wasn't as easy. And they needed all the time they could find to perfect their routines.

The team continued to debate what was causing the stomach bug. But by the time the team stretch was over, Rachel seemed optimistic. It didn't matter, she decided, what had caused the illness. They could overcome this.

"Sickness is a mindset," she shouted as the team filed out. "Just remember that."

. . .

Later that night, Leah texted the group about Olentangy's latest meet score, which the whole team had been keeping an eye out for. "146.9 for Berlin, you were right, Rachel," she wrote.

. . .

The team's stomach bug thankfully passed by the end of the week with only the four gymnasts catching it. Bailey, after two weeks of physical therapy, still wasn't ready to go for the district lineup. The coaches assured her it wasn't a problem and urged her not to rush back. Districts wasn't state meet, they said. State meet was the only thing that mattered. But districts was considered a dress rehearsal for it and a rare occasion they would be up against potentially some of their biggest competition: Medina, Hudson, and Brunswick. The team had a light practice before the district meet and when they finished, they gathered in front of Maria.

"I think the biggest thing going into Saturday is it's going to be tight," she told them. "Just being honest. No matter how great our meet is, it's still going to be tight. They're going to give us a run for our money, but we're not going to allow them to do that. I think of that 147 that we got, and we still didn't have a perfect meet.

"That should give you all so much hope on how much room we still can grow. We didn't have a perfect meet and got a 147. We had *far* from a perfect meet. We had many, many mistakes. Stuck dismounts that did not happen. Falls, leaps out of bounds. We have to just make sure that we clean all of that up. Every beam dismount should be stuck, every bar dismount should be stuck. All of those little tenths, that's going to set us apart.

"We can get eight-tenths back in our dismounts. And then we're already at a 148 and that's still counting GG's two falls that she had. So that puts us at a 149. So just think about how much potential we have and use that as your motivation going into it. We're not done at a 147. We're not even close to being done at a 147. We are capable of a 148 and above, and that's what we're going to do this weekend. Do not let anybody get in your way of that. You all have your focus sets. Keep that same stuff happening. We are good and we are going to do this no matter what happens.

"We're going to be there for each other, but we're going to be celebrating at the top."

CHAPTER 15

Districts

On Friday night, the Haverdills, Lea and Kyla's parents, arranged for the team to have a meditation session at a meditation and yoga studio near the gym. The team practiced breathing exercises to help calm themselves. And on Saturday at the district meet, things started well for the team on the bars. GG recovered from the shaken confidence of the previous two meets and stuck her landing for a 9.1. Rachel rocked her routine for a team-high 9.125, and Ella, Emily, and Lea all performed well with scores in the high 8s. Jeanne was the sixth competitor on the bars and she stood waiting for the okay to start her routine. Joan looked at her. "You've got this," she said. Jeanne smiled and nodded and then took to the bars. She nailed the first big move and then a second. The team went wild for each. Then she stuck the landing—9.075—exactly what they needed.

Rachel and Jeanne's scores were enough to qualify for the state meet individual competition in bars. For Addie, Jeanne's mom, it was a relief—and something special—to see after Jeanne's injuries during her first two years of high school.

"She's been struggling for a long time to get back to it," she said later. She ticked off all the times Jeanne had missed due to injuries. "I think she sat out four competitive club seasons. I mean she did maybe one or two things at a meet here or there, but I feel like it was two that she sat out completely, maybe did one event or one meet in the third year out. And then COVID came. It was years and years that she continued to go to the gym and wasn't competing."

To see her get back to a place where she could add new skills and qualify for the state meet as an individual was a special accomplishment after everything she'd fought through, Addie thought. Her injuries had started to hold her back in 2017. Six years later, she was still fighting. And now she was going to compete in the state meet.

. . .

Before beam, the gymnasts repeated the same meditation and model walk combination that got them in a good place at the sectional meet. They also incorporated some of the breathing exercises that they had learned the night before. It seemed to be working. There were four scores over 9.2: Rachel earned a 9.375, Emily a 9.250, Avery a 9.3, and GG a 9.3. GG's score, the coaches thought, was criminally low. The meet's head judge had even commented on how impressive she had been, which made Leah and Maria simultaneously happier and angrier about her score.

"GG's always been one of the top ones to look out for on paper, but beam was never really her forte last year," Leah said. "I know over summer she really worked hard on beam specifically to build that confidence up."

According to the head judge, GG should have gotten a 9.5 or a 9.6. "But I'll take a 9.3 any day," Leah said.

Ella had struggled a bit on hers—she messed up her lead pass and was short a jump so had to change her routine while on the beam. Beam routines were required to have certain elements. To compensate for mistakes, gymnasts had a list of backup skills that they practice and can be swapped in case of beam emergency. At the meet, Ella had to add in a split jump, which wasn't usually in her routine. She finished with a low-for-her score of 8.650. On floor, she finished with an 8.9. They weren't her best scores but not catastrophically bad—and she still had a chance to make it to the state meet individual competition for the fourth year in a row. As she approached vault, the last event of the day, with an all-around total of 26.475, Leah immediately could sense something was wrong. Ella normally scored a 9.2 on vault—she was a solid competitor at it. So before the event, Leah told her she needed to hit it to make it to the individual day of state meet.

But the pep talk backfired.

"She just put more pressure on herself to hit that score," Leah realized.

It was too much.

Her vault was off twice—and her best scored an 8.825. It was something that didn't matter for the team score, but meant that she wouldn't be competing on the second day of state meet.

Her face crumpled and she walked away from the vault and began to sob in the corner. Leah immediately understood and was thinking about how to rebuild her confidence going into the team day of state meet. "She's made all-around all three years, freshman, sophomore, and junior. You would think [in] your senior year you'd be the best that you could be. And right now, she's just not feeling that," she said.

Ella recovered soon after, though. It stung, sure, to not compete her senior year on individual day. She had a bad meet, but she had bad meets before. The team has had bad district meets before. And she was the team captain—and her focus, this year as it was all four years, was on taking another team state title.

That's the only thing that ever really mattered.

. . .

Tessa Brousek, the Padua gymnast, won the district all-around with a 38.2 score. Rachel came in behind for second with a 37.450 and GG at third with a 37.350. The team was feeling pretty good—their team score, a 147.950, was their highest of the season and more than a point above Medina's second-place finish.

"District Champs. Congrats to Medina, Brunswick, Hudson, Magnificat and Berea-Midpark teams for qualifying to states as well!" Leah wrote on Instagram. "Congrats to individual qualifiers:

Vault: GG, Rachel, Emily

Bars: Rachel, Jeanne

Beam: GG, Avery

Floor: GG, Rachel

AA: GG, Rachel, Emily

Ella, Delaney, Lea and Abby team contributors.

Congrats to Tessa from Padua- AA champ!"

#GoBees!!! Medina gymnastics wrote in the comments.

"Congrats ladies!!" wrote Olentangy Berlin Gymnastics' account.

Their joy was short-lived.

In Columbus, Olentangy Berlin had competed in a district meet of their own. "BEARS GYMNASTICS PLACES 1ST IN THE DISTRICT FOR THE THIRD YEAR IN A ROW BREAKING THE ALL TIME DISTRICT TEAM RECORD AND SCHOOL RECORD WITH A 148.8 TO QUALIFY FOR STATES!!!! #ClawsUp #BerlinPride #RoadtoStates4 #WeWill," the team tweeted.

Leah and Maria immediately started to think about how to make up the nearly one-point differential. Hours after the district meet ended, Maria sent a text to Emily and Jeanne. "Hey girls," she wrote. "Have you ever tried a switch leap Popa, switch side?" Emily responded: "I've tried them before but I think tour jete are easier for me, personally. With regards to the wolf full, I turn away from my leg that's straight which makes it difficult to get all the way around. I can try to do the switch side Popa or tour jete Popa on Tuesday.

"I've tried switch sides and I am really bad at them," Jeanne replied. "But I could try a switch half Popa because I think the wolf [turn] is my problem."

"Emily, love how you know why it is difficult," Maria responded. "Jeanne, let's try that." She added she was trying to come to practice Monday. "I can do a tour jete pretty well and make it all the way around but the second skill is my biggest challenge," Emily added. "We'll figure it out."

Jeanne kept trying to figure out how she could increase her score. "I've done double turns before but does that get any bonus?" she asked.

It didn't get the bonus, Emily responded, but it could still be helpful in increasing the score. Anything at this point to help, they'd take it.

Leah, Maria, and Jeanne had also made a decision about bars. Jeanne could compete her new routine on the second day of the state meet if she wanted, but for team day they were going to play it safe and go back to her old routine. "It's cleaner and she's more confident in it," Leah said.

Jeanne understood. She didn't really mind. She was just excited to be healthy enough to compete this year—and she knew they needed her scores to contribute in the top four.

CHAPTER 16

State Week

Just in case the team needed a reminder of what was coming in six days, Maria and Leah sent messages to the team group chat on Monday as school was letting out. "Have a great practice club girls," Maria wrote. "Work on dance skills floor beam bars—attack and clean up balance checks #makeitcount."

Leah quickly followed. "IT'S STATES WEEK BABY LFGGGGG!!! 20 on top."

And a second one. "I am PUMPED!!!!! Let's go out there and do the dang thing!!!" She added six trophy emojis.

A few hours later, they received their rotation for the state meet and Leah added one more. "THIRD FLIGHT BARS FOR THE BEES [bee emoji]." The order of events for teams at the state meet is chosen at random. The Bees were thrilled to hear they had an order that worked well for them—a good sign. First bars, then beam (they would be happy to get that out of the way early), then finishing on their strongest events—floor and vault.

Maria announced the exciting news to the parents.

Then Kim stepped in and laid out everything the parents were expected to do this week. "Yahoo! The girls made it to States! We have a busy and fun week. . . . . let's get the girls PUMPED UP!!!" she wrote. "Here is some information for the upcoming week:

- Signs will be displayed this week, we are still trying to find a spot (if you have any ideas or contacts for businesses that are near the center of town, please let us know)
- Captains will text the girls what to wear each day this week

- We need a volunteer to save seats at the state meet, please let Mark or Jen Evans know if you can do it

She then ticked down day by day what they were expected to do. It was a long list.

The most important thing that the parents did for state week was to decorate the team bus for a send-off. On Wednesday night, the parents gathered for three hours at Ella's house to work on posters, personalized gifts, and other decorations. "We will also be painting a banner for the girls for the send off as well," Kim wrote in an email before the event. "Please bring your donations then or you are welcome to drop off at my house or with Ella. Please bring your own scissors and if you have a hot glue gun and some glue, we could use a couple more."

After that gathering, their plan was to gather early Friday morning to decorate before the team had to get on the road. "Good morning!" one parent wrote Thursday morning. "It was suggested that we share some photos of last year's bus decorations so you know what to expect tomorrow morning if you are helping to decorate. Please bring tape with you. We have limited time to get everything in place so it is a frenzy with everyone on the bus doing something! We will start with freshmen at the front of the bus and work backwards. Please tell your gymnast NOT to remove any decorations from the bus & seats except for their picture—we hope to be able to reuse some items and this will help us keep track of everything. Mel Kirin will be removing all decorations from the bus upon return to the gym on Saturday. If you will be there to pick up your gymnast, I'm sure she would welcome extra hands to get everything down quickly! Thanks to everyone for your donations and help throughout the season [smiley face emoji]."

The photos showed each seat on the bus decorated with a black plaid blanket, a large yellow laminated *B* with a pink gymnast on it, photos of each girl's gift bags, small flags lining the bus, and cutouts on the window that said BEES on the top and STATEBOUND on the bottom.

The team coordinated outfits every day of the week going into the state meet. On Monday, they wore shirts supporting another team's gymnast that had been diagnosed with leukemia. Tuesday, they dressed up. Wednesday was competition leos. Thursday was the state meet shirt. The purpose was to stand out and remind their peers that they were competing for a state title—again. "For me, because I'm a senior, most people [I see] already know the traditions but the freshmen definitely get a lot of questions," Ella said.

Delaney painstakingly, as per tradition, made hair bows for each of the girls to be put in the goodie bags on the bus. They were black bows with red on top, a layer of black and gold spotted ribbon, with gold and red crisscrossing on top. Ribbon with blue dots held it together. Putting them together was one of the most stressful parts of her week.

Reporters from the local Cleveland news stations had been at practice that week, putting out reports focusing on the Bees going for their twentieth state title—a dynasty, one reported breathlessly, was bigger than any of the other classic ones in the area. "As my dad used to say, we don't rebuild, we reload," Maria told the local TV station WKYC reporter Nick Camino. "So we're hoping we've reloaded enough to stay on top of that award stand. The girls have done a great job this year."

"Sometimes when I'm at home and I'm not doing anything, I think about the legacy that we're a part of right now," Ella added in the report. "And I hope I'm able to tell my kids about how I won four years."

In the report, Nick Camino said he was confident that the twentieth year would be just like the previous nineteen. He ended the report with a prediction: "I don't think anyone is doubting this dynasty won't end anytime soon."

. . .

Bailey was sitting in class at school on the Thursday before state meet when she was pinged in a group text with Maria and Leah. Avery was sick. That meant they were going to try to have her fill in at that afternoon's state practice run-through at beam. Would she be up for it? She glanced down at her still-swollen ankle.

Of course, she replied.

She didn't tell them how stressed she had been the week leading into states, just trying to do everything she could for her ankle. She had been going to physical therapy every weekday with Melissa Haverdill, Lea and Kyla's mom. They had been working on getting the swelling down and slowly easing into jumping and landing. She figured that she only needed to grit through it a few times—the pain would be worth the state title. And she didn't let on to her coaches how much it was still hurting.

So when she found out that Avery might be sidelined and they needed her to fill in on beam, she wasn't about to tell them. "I obviously want to do this to help out the team because it's important to me," she said. "Everyone has the same goal in mind with states, so I'm going to do anything to help that."

She was determined.

She really just wanted to do it for the team. "Not just do it for myself," she said. "But do it for everyone."

. . .

Right before school dismissed for the day, the gymnasts walked through the halls past the trophy case dedicated to Ron Ganim as the Brecksville-Broadview Heights marching band played around them for a "clap out." The Bees parents and school administrators gathered to wish them well.

Two hours away, at Olentangy Berlin, the gymnasts followed the school cheerleaders through the hallway as their classmates and teachers applauded them. *The Columbus Dispatch,* their local newspaper, had a story headlined "Tayten Swain, Olentangy Berlin Set Sights on OHSAA Gymnastics All-Around, Team Titles." The article pointed out that Brecksville had nineteen consecutive titles, but, Frank DiRenna wrote:

> However, Berlin's score of 148.85 at district set program and meet records and topped Brecksville's first-place effort (147.95) in the Northeast District meet Saturday at Hudson.
>
> "This team has the potential," Hedrick told the newspaper. "I am just hoping we are able to stay healthy and uninjured this week. It should be a good show at the state meet. All these gymnasts are so talented and motivated. I know they will bring their A game."

It was too late for the Bees to worry. After the clap out, they went straight to Gym World for one last walk-through.

At practice there was a nervous, giddy type of energy. In less than twelve hours, they'd be boarding the buses for Columbus. Joan and Maria walked through the entrance of the gym, carrying some equipment to the back. "I'm more nervous," Joan said about the state meet than usual. Maria nodded. "My anxiety is through the roof," she said.

Avery's illness didn't help either. Joan looked at the snacks spread out on the table in front of her. "Nobody is to touch the cookies until they wash their hands," she said, mostly to herself. The gymnasts weren't in the room to hear her. "And even after you do, you can only touch the one you eat."

Joan also worried about how many people were traveling to see them at the state meet in support of the potential twentieth consecutive title. Any small changes in anything at the state meet—including the supporters that came to cheer them on—she worried would upset whatever luck they had going for them. "My sons are both going and I'm saying 'No you're not jinxing us,'" she said. "The superintendent, she always comes down but she's staying the night. Alecia Farina, she and her mother are driving down. And I'm wondering, really? I guess that's good . . . she's coming to support us. I mean we always get a lot of people, a lot of alumni. But usually I don't always know who's up there until after the meet. I'm not going to worry about it now."

"We'll get through it," she added later. "We will."

But first, the walk-through.

Abby looked nervous. She walked over to Maria. "Mrs. Schneider," she said. "Do you know if I'm going to vault at states yet?" Maria didn't have an answer. With less than a day to go, they were still working through variables of the vault lineup. "We don't know yet," she said. "So you're going to vault today."

Abby nodded and walked over to the vault area where she spent most of the practice going through her approach.

The Lil Uzi Vert song "Better Days" blasted through Gym World as the gymnasts got ready to start practice.

"Let's go," Maria said, clapping. "I'd love to get out of here by 4:20." That meant going for a perfect walk-through with everyone hitting their routines confidently.

Bailey came over to ask Maria what she should be practicing. Maria pointed again to Avery's illness and that there might be a hole in the lineup at beam. "You had one of the top scores before you were hurt, so we believe in you," she said. Bailey nodded. The two discussed it a little more.

"I might just go on low beam and try it out," she said. Maria agreed that was a good idea. "Because again number one priority is vault because your score could be counted there."

Bailey walked over to the low beam. She did a standing bend tuck to test her ankle. Instantly, she grimaced in pain and doubled over.

Maria looked alarmed. She knew she had made a costly mistake. "Forget that then," she said.

Bailey went to the side. She would try again tomorrow. She just had to battle through it for one vault. She could do it, she thought. She had to.

Trying not to show how much of a disaster she thought Bailey's injury was, Maria turned back to the team. "We're fine," she said, her stomach turning.

Joan watched as Emily practiced her beam routine, offering some last-minute tips. The coaches knew that Emily was going to be a factor in the state meet before she even started high school, but what they always worried most about was her confidence. They didn't want to coach her too much. "Press down, feel the beam, Emily," she said. "Don't rush. Press down on that back foot. Press down."

She looked over at Tessa Brousek, who would be competing on the second day of the state meet as an individual. "Don't kick that leg so high, 45-degree angle or you don't get credit," she said.

Tessa nodded. "Yeah," she replied quickly.

Joan looked back at Emily. "You're bending forward instead of snapping your legs. Snap it."

Then later: "Smile out there," she said. "Show it off. Remember every corner you go to out there there's going to be a judge, so smile."

A bit quieter, Joan corrected herself, "They're actually going to be in the middle."

The song quickly changed to the Nicki Minaj and 2 Chainz song "Beez in the Trap," one of the team's unofficial theme songs as the gymnasts cheered Ella as she started on doing her bars routine. GG was next; hers looked good. Lea followed. "Good, come on, Lea!" Leah shouted. "Come on, Lea! Come on Lea!"

She stuck her landing.

"Don't be nervous, be aggressive and know that you're going to make it," Leah told her.

They finished six for six on bars. Next up, beam.

"Guys, it's going to come down to every dismount, every stuck routine," Leah said.

Jeanne was put back into the lineup. The team had gone five for five when she stepped up. It wasn't her best routine. She fell a few minutes earlier practicing as well, and was frustrated with herself. "Gosh, that was so bad," she said. Leah tried to remind her that she could do beam—even if she hadn't been planning on it at the state meet until now. She had competed in it off and on all season. "You're better than that," Leah said. "It's going to be loud, it's going to be crazy, and you have to be ready to go in at any moment. And that goes for everyone."

Then floor. Emily was first—"Come on, Em!" her teammates shouted. On cue, midway through the routine, they shouted together: "Brecksville, Broadview Heights, Bees!" and clapped. "Come on, Em!" they continued. "You got this!"

"Come on, keep your feet together," Leah said.

She was doing great. But then, at the end, she fell. She lay on the floor, laughing.

"Emily, if you would do that in the meet, stay down, make it look like that's the move. Roll," Joan said.

"Fake it," Leah said.

Then came Jeanne. Immediately, Joan had an order: "SMILE," she said.

The team cheered. "Come on, Jeanne!" they yelled.

It was a good rehearsal. They could move on. Then Delaney—with the same instructions from Joan: "Smileeee," she said.

The team clapped together and shouted "Bees!"

She finished her routine and the team cheered. Leah gave some last-minute pointers. Ella was up next—the team clapped in sync at the beginning and twice more in her routine. The year before, in the individual portion of the meet, she had scored a 9.35 to come in eighth overall.

"Squeeze your legs on that tumbling pass," Joan said.

Rachel was next. She made it through her first pass. "YES, KELLY!" Leah shouted.

The team alternated between claps, "Yes, Kelly!" and "Let's go!"

When she finished, the coaches and gymnasts broke into applause. "Good job, Kel!" Leah said.

Joan called her over for a quick tip on her leap. GG was last. "PRESS ON THAT BIG TOE!" Joan shouted to her. The team continued to cheer. "Bees!" they said in sync to end her routine, and then all applauded. Six for six.

They finished the day with vault—with Bailey out, it was Abby, Ella, Emily, Rachel, GG, and Lea.

At the end of practice, the team gathered as Maria led them in a meditation. "Lay down. Even if you're not competing you can still lay down and close your eyes because you're going to have a role tomorrow too. In through your nose, out through your mouth with your breathing. Getting our way to tomorrow. Alright, we're going to load that bus. We're going to get down to Columbus. We're going to enjoy a beautiful lunch together. Go to our rooms. Hopefully, all will be ready. We'll get all pertied up. Get on the bus. Head to Hilliard Bradley. When we get there, it's going to be calming. Not calming. Just kidding. We're third flight bars tomorrow. If you're an individual like Tessa, think of yourself going Saturday. Starting on bars, flight feet. So let's start on bars. We're going to have a nice warm-up. If you're competing in that event, think of going through your routine, what needs to happen in warm-up for you. What's your role if you're not competing that event? Make it count in your head as you envision what you're doing.

"First warm-up event is done. We're going to walk through that tunnel. We're going to hear all the fans cheering nice and loud. It's wild, it's crazy. It's something like you freshies have never seen. We're going to get started on bars.

"Go ahead and envision and walk through that bar routine, what it's supposed to feel like. Every body part, every muscle, start to finish from recitation to saluting to presenting at the end. Go ahead and do a bar routine."

She paused for a minute.

"We are going to head over to beam as our next warm-up. We get a little break, a little pause in the day. We'll have a little bit of a break and then we'll start warming up beam.

"We come out to beam on the other side of the gym from the bars, we're going to go through our beam routines, start to finish. What does it feel like? Present to the judge. Sticky feet at the end. STB. Make it count, every move on that beam right now."

She paused again. The noise from the gymnastics classes going on downstairs filtered through the meditation.

"Beam is done."

"We're moving on. Fun events. We get to show off. Now, when we're on floor performing from start to finish, I want you to feel every one of those movements. Now do your floor routine."

She paused again.

"How are we going to be remembered on that floor when you're done performing?

"Now moving on to the vault. Yeah, Leah's at the end of that vault, ready to go crazy. At the back end, Mrs. G [is] making sure we have the right numbers up. Go ahead and go through your two vaults, how that's going to feel from start to finish there. What's your role? If you're not on vault, for the team, how are you going to be there for your teammates? How loud are you going to be? Obnoxious. We're going to be obnoxious."

The team lay still for a few more moments and then opened their eyes. They got up to gather their things up. "We got this, girls," Maria said. "Positive mindsets MAKE. It. Count."

"And let's do the damn thing," Leah added.

Maria then turned it over to her mom.

"Are you ready?" she asked the girls, her voice loud, hopeful, and cheery.

"YEAH," they said back, giggling and semi enthused.

"You are the worst cheerleaders," Joan said. "You're supposed to go YEAH!"

"Go again," Rachel said.

"ARE YOU READY?"

"YEAH!" they replied, a little better this time.

Practice was officially over.

"Make good choices tonight," Maria said. "Get good sleep."

"Lucky chicken," Leah said, referencing the chicken in Ella's parents' freezer and the dinner that they were going to at the same restaurant that night.

Even with the disappointing chicken of the year prior, it was tradition. And they couldn't break tradition. But at dinner that night, there was a hiccup with the lucky chicken: the restaurant wasn't serving the same chicken dish. The gymnasts had to opt for chicken parmesan.

But then, they thought about it a little more.

Was the lucky chicken even lucky? After all, they thought the streak was over after the final event of the meet. While they won, they didn't want a repeat of the drama that came along with it. Lucky chicken, it was decided, was not actually lucky at all. So after a full year of keeping it, Ella reached into the back of the freezer at her house and threw it in the trash.

This threw the whole concept of the lucky chicken in question. If the lucky chicken wasn't lucky, the replacement lucky chicken parmesan wasn't lucky either, they decided. So the next morning, there was no lucky chicken as the gymnasts gathered at Gym World to go to the state meet.

"We didn't bring it because we were all scared that we were going to fall on beam if we brought it because last year we—" Ella started to say.

Another gymnast shushed her.

"Never mind," Ella said.

. . .

Mostly due to the intense amount of superstitions that overtook the entire Brecksville-Broadview Heights team, their coaches, and their parents by the day of the state meet, everything went according to time-honored, long-repeated, and highly respected tradition.

On Friday morning, the team gathered at Gym World, as their parents scrambled outside to get a good exit going. "No stealing toilet paper," Joan reminded them, anticipating the potential celebration that could happen at the end of the weekend if everything went well. The team gathered in the lobby of Gym World, double-checking equipment. "What am I forgetting?" Rachel said. "I feel like I'm forgetting something."

"A 9.6 in your back pocket for vault?" Leah asked.

"I don't actually have back pockets," Rachel said. "I only have side pockets."

"Well, good, a 9.5 for floor, a 9.6 for vault," Leah said.

"Got it," Rachel said. "A 9.4 on beam."

"9.3 on bars," Leah added.

A smoke machine was set up in front of the Gym World entrance and Ella's dad Matt stood next to the bus with a microphone. "CLEVELAND!" he shouted, in his best arena announcer impression. "You wanted the best? You've got the best. The hottest team in the world. BEEEEES!"

"Just Wanna Rock" played as the gymnasts walked out of the gym and onto the bus, most of them looking more bemused than energized. "BE!" the parents shouted. "ES! BE, ES!" They cheered. The bus had been meticulously decorated by the parents and the bus driver, Maria learned, had a connection to the team: Her granddaughter had once competed on the team. It was a good start to the day.

A police escort drove the team the first few miles on the two-hour drive to Columbus, a straight shot on I-71. The parents drove home briefly or went and got breakfast before making their way behind it. The day was here.

CHAPTER 17

States

Even the Bees' parents closely followed the state meet day traditions. Hours after sending the bus off, a group of parents gathered in the hotel lobby getting ready to go to Beer Barrel Pizza and Grill, the place Bees' parents always went for lunch. Avery and her mom walked in, hustling to get out of the still-pouring rain. On Wednesday night, Avery realized she didn't feel well but tried to get a good night's sleep and hoped it would help. When she woke up early the next morning, she had a sinking feeling: She still felt bad. "It was terrible," her mom said. "We didn't know what was going on and we were just hopeful and prayed that it was a twenty-four-hour thing and maybe she missed practice." Avery couldn't believe her bad luck. States was supposed to be the culminating moment of the season—and she was supposed to be in the lineup. She took a COVID test. It came back negative. Then she texted Maria and Leah to let them know what was going on. "They told me to rest up and obviously if I didn't feel good, not to compete, but obviously I wanted to compete," she said. "I just rested the whole day and took a lot of medicine and fluids and by Thursday my temperature was down."

She missed the team dinner and the morning send-off. To be safe, the coaches and Avery agreed she should drive down separately. But when she walked into the hotel lobby, she had good news: She was fine. She could compete. The parents in the lobby cheered and she went off to find her team.

. . .

After the gymnasts ate lunch at the hotel (as they always did), the team gathered in each other's rooms to braid their hair. Each gymnast had her own superstitions attached to this part of the day as well. Sometime throughout the season, the girls divided into two groups: The group that was good at braiding hair and the group that needed help. Then they piled into rooms at the hotel and made sure everyone's hair was done appropriately. Rachel texted Jeanne days before each meet to reserve her braiding services. "She just said anytime I do it, she always has a good meet so I have to do it," Jeanne said. Jeanne also did Bailey's hair. Carol and Delaney were also go-to braiding artists on the team. "It changes each year," Jeanne added of the designated hair experts. "Last year Lindsay and Erin did it. You pass it down to people."

The hairstyles were all two braids in the back and then piled up into a bun.

Ella had worn "space buns" (her curly hair pulled up in a bun on either side of her head) in the postseason so far, a hairstyle that brought her luck in previous years. But she made the decision to change it after what happened at districts. With hair and makeup finished, the gymnasts gathered in the hotel lobby, lingering inside looking at the rain as they waited for the bus. "What do they say about rain on your wedding day?" Joan asked out loud.

Rachel responded: "We're marrying that trophy."

A few minutes later, Rachel looked at her phone.

"It's 2:22, make a wish," she exclaimed.

"Win states," someone shouted back.

The team piled onto the bus for a short bus ride to Hilliard Bradley High School. Leah and Maria sat silently in the front, nervously typing on their phones. Lea turned The Black Eyed Peas' song that had become one of their favorites on her boom speakers. Rachel, Lea, Kyla, and Bailey started singing along in the back of the bus to "Beez in the Trap," then switched to a few lines of Wiz Khalifa's "Black and Yellow."

"Am I allowed to put a song request in?" Leah asked. "'We Get Turnt Up.' It's a good one."

Lea nodded and the group in the back of the bus continued to sing the Jay Z/Kanye West and Rihanna song "Run This Town" and giggled. If they were tense, it wasn't showing outwardly yet. Leah's song came on and they sang and clapped along.

The songs continued. Leah looked over at Maria. "I feel like I black out until this bus ride," she said. "I just feel like every time at states, I don't even realize it until I'm on this bus ride. Well, obviously I feel nervous about it. It feels like we just did this."

The track switched to "Girls Just Want to Have Fun." "I know this one!" Maria said proudly.

A few minutes later, Maria wanted to check in another good luck charm: A bottle of honey that Leah bought that morning from the grocery store. It was meant cheekily to be in response to Olentangy's mascot, the Bears. Leah declared that morning that it was a token of luck they had to guard at all times. "Who's got the honey?" Maria shouted.

"Where's the honey?" Leah shouted.

One of the gymnasts raised it proudly.

"Yeah!" Maria yelled. "Protect that honey!"

"PTH," Leah added.

As the bus pulled into the school driveway, Leah tried to direct the bus driver to the correct entrance. "Medina" she said, as she looked out the window. "Right in front of us. Oh my god—someone who is dressed as a legitimate bee just ran past us." The gymnasts looked out the window and saw the backed-up line to check in. It was a huge potential problem, they complained, since they all had just spent hours on their hair. And even to get to the entrance to stand in that line was a long walk.

There was no choice, though.

They tried to get everything as organized as they could before braving it. "Goooo Bees," Joan said as they got off the bus and tried to get inside as quickly as possible.

"Oh my god oh my god oh my god oh my god," one gymnast said as the group ran into the gym.

"I can't see," added another as the rain pelted on her.

When the Bees finally got into the auxiliary gym, there were signs on the wall designating where each team should put their things. They walked over and dropped their backpacks and loads of snacks and began to look around. The Medina Bee mascot wandered around nearby and came over to snap pictures with the Brecksville Bees. There were a lot of familiar faces—the gymnasts mingled and said hi to some of their friends on the other teams. Maria, as per her tradition, went to a small makeshift souvenir store opened at the state meet in the cafeteria and bought a state T-shirt for each of the gymnasts.

Maria and Leah went to a coaches' meeting, then all twelve teams went into the gym for a grand entrance and to line up for the "Star Spangled Banner." The Bees were in the third rotation. They had some time to sit around in the back gym and get warmed up and try to relax before their first event, bars.

Bars was a good event to start the meet with. It was a difficult one, but not their worst event. Emily was up first. The gym was divided into four quadrants—bars were on the side closest to the door leading into the hallway next to the auxiliary gym. The mat for floor exercise was ahead and to the right. Throughout the competition, gymnasts had to ignore the music that went along with each floor routine and echoed through the gym. Ahead and to the left was the vault. And all the way on the other side was beam. Spectators were in bleachers and the Bees' supporters gathered into an area midway in the upper bleachers, packed tightly in with their scorebooks and cheering accessories ready.

At the start of each flight, each team was introduced as they walked through the side door of the gym. The whole team walked together, regardless of who was competing. It was a mini parade every time, as the gymnasts nervously congregated in groups, sometimes quickly flitting back and forth for last-minute good wishes to friends on other teams.

Just as they did at every meet, the Bees gymnasts gathered to the side of the uneven bars to cheer on Emily. She earned a 9.125. A great start. GG was next. Leah and Maria moved her up in the rotation after her falls earlier in the postseason. They figured it would take a little bit of pressure off and hoped it would stop her from losing focus or confidence while watching her teammates compete before her. It worked—she earned a 9.275. Lea was up next, earning a 9.125. Then Rachel, with the same score. Ella, competing her last bar routine as a Bee, an event that she had been one of the best at in the state for four years, earned a 9.225. Jeanne was the last in the group. A few moments into her routine, she fell. It wasn't the way she wanted to start, especially after all the work she had put into the event and everything she had overcome. But it was fine. Only the top four scores counted—and the first five were more than enough to carry the team. The team total was 36.750—only .125 less than last season.

The team filed into the back auxiliary gym and turned their focus. Next came beam. They did model walks to relax. When it was time to go in, the gymnasts lined up and walked into the hallway where Ella led them in a meditation. Lea led off. As she took her turn, the other five gathered in the side hallway. She earned an 8.9. Then GG, a 9.025. Ella, despite the coach's advice not to, strained to listen from the hallway. Even though the whole point of being out there was to not know how it was going, it was impossible to not wonder. She heard cheers, but it was hard to tell where they were coming from. She walked in for her turn. A 9.2. Then Emily, a 9.15. That meant four gymnasts went—and no one fell. A complete reversal of last year. "One more, one more," Joan mouthed to Maria. Avery competed fifth, earning a 9.0. Rachel was up last, but when her turn came up, she couldn't be found. The coaches and her teammates looked around for her before hearing a pounding on the back door. She was locked out of the gym. She laughed and managed to not let it affect her routine, tying with Ella for a team-high 9.2.

The team gathered in a circle next to the beam. They had vanquished the bad whatever of last year. "Six for six," Maria yelled. They were cautiously ecstatic.

They hit eleven of twelve routines. But they were still in third place—.85 behind Olentangy Berlin and .275 behind Medina going into the last two events.

The Bees went back to the auxiliary gym to wait for their third event, floor. Lea blasted some Soulja Boy on her speaker and they had a brief dance party as the other teams completed their events to get to the halfway mark of the meet.

. . .

Ella knew her team had to bring it all on floor exercise, one of their strongest events. She gathered the gymnasts who were competing—Emily, Jeanne, Delaney, Rachel, and GG—in for a quick huddle and a brief pep talk.

Emily was up first. The team lined up on the side, cheering and yelling "Brecksville Bees!" at the correct spot. She earned a 9.2. Then came Jeanne. A 9.375. Delaney, who fought for four years to earn this spot in the state meet, stumbled momentarily in her routine. Leah was quickly in her face. "Let's GO" she shouted. Delaney's face snapped back and she refocused and completed her routine, earning a 9.4. Ella was next—the team clapped in unison during her routine—and she earned a 9.35. They rushed into a circle around her to celebrate. Up next was Rachel—she had a bad warm-up and then fell during her routine. She tried to bounce back, but it was too much to overcome in her score—she earned an 8.875. It was fine. They had four scores before her that could be counted for a comfortable final total. And then came GG—she anchored the team with a team-high 9.525. The team score was 37.650—.2 points lower than the year before. But their beam score had been 36.575, more than a point higher than they had scored last year.

The count for the team was good at this point: They hit sixteen of eighteen routines. They should be in a great spot.

But they were still in third place.

CHAPTER 18

"Get Yourself over That Horse Right Now"

The Brecksville-Broadview Heights coaches tried to keep their team focused on themselves, so they discouraged the gymnasts from tracking other teams' scores at the state meet. That job of tracking scores of other teams traditionally fell to the parents, who were sitting on the spectator bleachers in the main gym, far away from the team. This year, Delaney's dad started a shared notes document where the parents compiled scores and tracked as a group. Down on the floor, Maria, Leah, and Joan were able to view it too on their phones. And like always, the coaches swapped scores with teams through quick side conversations.

Throughout the meet, the parents and coaches had their eyes on three teams. The first was Brunswick, the rival that pressed the Bees' buttons all season. Then Medina, a team coached by a Gym World alum and whose gymnasts were friendly with Brecksville's gymnasts. And third was Delaware Olentangy Berlin, the team in Columbus that had been on their radar all season.

As the team sat in the auxiliary gym waiting for vault, their final event, Maria and Leah did mental calculations. The meet was close. The good news: After being in third all meet, they were .75 ahead of Medina going into the final round. But the bad news: They were .25 behind Delaware Olentangy Berlin.

Leah sent a text message to Alecia Farina, the former Brecksville gymnast and current Gym World coach who had come to Columbus to support her former team. "I need a hug," Leah said.

Alecia came to the auxiliary gym to try to loosen their nerves. Maria snuck out to watch Olentangy Berlin in their last event, the uneven bars, to see just what the Brecksville team would need going into the last event. It didn't help. Olentangy Berlin had their best day on bars of the season. Maria looked sick. "This is absolutely ridiculous," she said under her breath, as she walked in the gym.

The first two Olentangy Berlin gymnasts scored below a 9. But then came a 9.425—higher than any of the Brecksville gymnasts had gotten in the event. Then a 9.225. And a 9.3. Their final score was 148.050, higher than Brecksville had scored all season.

Maria's heart sank. Back in the auxiliary gym, the bad news kept coming.

Bailey, with a wrapped ankle and a lot of determination, tried to go for a warm-up vault and couldn't do it. The ankle that she had injured in the conference championship on her first event and tweaked the day before in practice still hurt too much to go. She was devastated. Earlier that day, she woke up and figured the adrenaline would kick in enough to get her through the state meet. "It's only a couple of vaults," she had thought. "I can push through it. Meet adrenaline will kick in."

But when she started warming up before the final event, it was too much. "There's no way," she thought. She told her coaches, and then walked away from the warm-up area and started to cry. Quickly, Kyla and Carol went to comfort her. She kept walking, heading back toward the other side of the gym, trying to quarantine herself from the rest of the team's warm-ups, with tears coming uncontrollably. She felt like she was letting the team down. And the questions kept running through her mind: What if this costs us states? And what if this costs her her career with the Bees? What if she never earns her lineup spot back? "I'm afraid for next year they won't have trust in me and won't put me in because I cracked under pressure," she thought.

Maria felt awful. It was her fault, she thought, for asking Bailey to try beam in practice. She wanted to know if Bailey could do beam as an insurance policy if Avery wasn't better, and it turned out that it was too much pressure on her ankle too quickly. Now they were without a vault they likely needed. Bailey's concerns that she wouldn't be counted on in future meets and seasons was ridiculous, she told her. "It's not your fault," she reassured the teary-eyed freshman.

That left Lea as the sixth person in the lineup. The junior was a skilled, experienced gymnast, but her best vault wasn't going to be above a 9 because of its difficulty level.

Despite the coaches' efforts to keep their team focused on themselves, the news from the competition gym about Berlin's bars scores circulated through the team. The gymnasts had a lot of time between events, which meant they spent it on their phones, eating snacks, surrounded by their bags against the wall in the auxiliary gym. So it was pretty easy to keep track of the meet even if they weren't supposed to.

They did the math. They needed a 9.3 average on vault to win. That would be a higher average than anyone else had had at the meet so far. But it was doable: The week before Emily had scored a 9.65, GG had gotten a 9.625, and Rachel earned a 9.5. They'd need Ella and Abby to hit their vaults in addition to the top three hitting their scores. There was no room for error.

This was the make or break time for keeping the nineteen-year streak going. Outwardly, Rachel was confident. "We do that," she said aloud of the 9.3 average to the group. "We do that."

Maria wasn't the only one who didn't want the news to spread. Ella's stomach grew tighter in knots when she heard. She wished no one had told her. "I'm the type of person that doesn't like to know, but apparently everyone on the team does," she said. Despite Rachel's brave face, Ella felt her nerves surging. "Confident we could do it, but also super nervous," she said. Abby stood silently away from the team, practicing her run-up steps to herself. She looked petrified.

As the time came for them to line up and walk into the gym for vault, the team circled up and danced around the boom speaker. Then, for the last time of the meet, it was their turn to walk into the gym. Hudson was on bars, Perrysburg on beam, and Berea-Midpark on floor. Leah felt like she was having an out-of-body experience as she walked into the gym. Everyone had their eyes on the Bees. The whole gym knew that the title was theirs to lose and history, either way the meet went, was about to be made.

. . .

In the 2022 championship meet, the last-minute warm-ups before the event were the first sign that things were going to go badly on the beam, the last event of that meet. And this year, warm-ups for the last event were no better. This year they were in a more precarious position.

Unlike the year prior, the Bees were the ones chasing the first-place team—not the team trying to hold onto their lead. They looked tight. No one could stick their landing. Leah tried to get her team to calm down. As the gymnasts warmed up, she put her hands on each of their shoulders and looked at them. "You can do this," she said.

Abby was first. She didn't know all week if she was going to be in the lineup, but now she was starting at the season's biggest moment. A little more than a week before, she'd not been able to land her vault, leaving her with a score that could have sunk the Bees if she did it this week and they needed it to count as one of the top four.

She took a deep breath, ran and took off, and hit her landing. 8.9.

In high school gymnastics, gymnasts were given two tries at the vault, with the higher score counted. Abby decided to go for it again to see if she could boost her score.

She didn't hit it. But 8.9 was what they counted on her for. It was a good start. She was ecstatic. She had been put into the lineup to set the tone and she felt like she succeeded. "We came up with this thing last year where we have six people go at an event and each person has a job of some sort," she said later. "The first person's job was to set the table, second person was the appetizer person, the third person's job was to eat the entrée. Fourth person was dessert, fifth person was clear the table, and sixth person would do the dishes.

"I set the table. Yeah, that's pretty cool."

Watching in the stands, Janelle, her mom, thought it was the perfect moment. She tended to hide and pace when either of her kids were in stressful situations in sports. So as Abby prepared to vault, Janelle stood by herself at the opposite end of the gym, videotaping and hoping for the best. She was so nervous that her hands were shaking. When Abby hit her first vault, ensuring a good start for the team, tears of pride and relief began flowing out. She sprinted back across the gym to join the rest of the parents.

"I can't express in words the sheer happiness I felt that she had finally achieved what she had worked so hard to do for the past three years," Janelle said later. "Her score didn't matter to me. All I cared about was that she hit that vault. I'll never forget that moment."

Abby had done her job.

Then came Ella, in her last event as a high school gymnast. She had had a good meet so far, but the pressure in this moment was unreal: It was her senior year. If Brecksville lost, it would be (at least in her head) her name highlighting the part in the record books that she had captained the team that lost. And, in the district meet the week before, she had a bad vault that cost her a spot in the second day of the state meet.

Ella started her run. But her steps were off, so she stopped. A false start. Then another one. She had one chance left. Maria was apoplectic. She looked into Ella's panicked eyes. "You have done this vault. You could do this vault in your sleep," she told her. "What is going on?"

"I don't know," Ella said. "I'm just stopping."

Maria didn't know what to say. "Figure it out," she said. "Get yourself over that horse right now."

Before the event started, Ella's dad Matt had left his spot in the parents' section in the stands to get closer to the floor and try to take a few pictures. He wanted to be able to celebrate his daughter's last vault as a Bee. All of a sudden, he started to worry. In a matter of seconds, he went from being worried about whether she was going to win the championship to worried about the mental well-being of his daughter. He started thinking about Simone Biles, dropping out of the Olympics. He started to think about the enormity of the moment, especially in his daughter's life as a Brecksville gymnast. He started to wonder what she would be feeling if she somehow couldn't get over this vault, one he had seen her do hundreds of times before. "Please," he thought, "don't let this happen to my daughter."

Leah's mind was spinning. She had coached Ella in this event since middle school. She had watched her do it perfectly hundreds of times. And she had never seen someone have a block like this in the middle of the most important moment at a state meet.

Rachel's confidence began to waiver. "If she doesn't hit her next vault, that's it," she thought. "That's the streak."

Ella had one try left.

She took a deep breath, stared ahead, and she went again.

"Let's go, Ella!" her teammates yelled in sync.

Lea would say later that Ella's steps looked off. But she did a round-off onto the table and a back pike off.

She stuck the landing. 9.125.

Ella's mom Kim jumped out of her seat in celebration. The team cheered and collectively started to breathe again, but their faces remained tense.

Next came Emily. The freshman's vault was a Yurchenko layout, one of the toughest routines on the team. She sprinted down, did a roundoff onto the sprint board, backspring onto the vault table, and a straight body flip to the mat.

9.45.

Then Rachel, who had been unable to compete her vault until recently. "The trophy's right there," she thought. I just have to do my part."

First try a 9.45. Then a 9.55. "That's it," she thought to herself. "That's meet."

Good, but they still needed one more. It all lay on GG, the sophomore. The sixth vaulter didn't have a vault with a high enough score to secure them the win. They needed GG to stick her vault or the streak was likely done.

GG was one of the best vaulters in the state. But her usual quiet confidence wavered at points this season. The ill-timed stomach bug had thrown her off her game, and two weeks earlier she slipped off the uneven bars at the sectional tournament and scored in the low 8s. The continuation of a nineteen-year streak that honored the beloved coaches of her club gym and the dozens of other gymnasts it represented depended on her making this vault.

And most of the hundreds of people watching in that gym wanted her to miss. Gymnasts walked through the hall on the side of the gym, whispering about the close score, trying to catch a glimpse. The crowd was eerily quiet.

The rest of the meet had concluded. The three teams who were already out on the floor for the final grouping remained there, watching the Bees compete. Jen, the Olentangy Berlin coach, had avoided looking at the scores for the entire meet. She was stunned as she walked out when her team finished their events and learned that they were leading Brecksville. But she wasn't counting on anything. "They're really strong on vault," her daughter had reminded her. "That's where they're going to get us." Above the gymnasts in the stands, all the parents were focused on GG too. GG just looked at it in the simplest terms. "I just have to hit this," she thought.

Her vault was identical to Emily's—Yurchenko layout.

Fifteen years ago, Leah stood there as a Brecksville gymnast with her team needing a 9.7 vault score to win. But then the streak was only a few years old and her teammate, Andrea, was a senior at the time. Standing in a similar spot, this time as a coach, waiting for another difficult vault to save the streak a lifetime later, Leah flashed back to that moment and thought about how much worse it felt to be on the coaching side. She felt helpless. The year before, as she watched her team fall off of beam repeatedly and their lead shrink, she had apologized to Joan. That year, she finally realized what she and her friends had put the Ganims through as coaches when Leah was a gymnast in high school. The feeling was terrible.

As GG took a deep breath, a line of Brecksville gymnasts stood by the runway cheering. The Brecksville parents were standing in their seats, fifteen feet above in the bleachers. Behind her, Maria, Lea, and Joan yelled encouragement from the start of the runway. Leah, Ella, Rachel, and Jeanne stood at the end, yelling as loudly as they could. GG sprinted down, did her roundoff onto the sprint board, backspring onto the vault table, and a straight body flip to the mat.

"It was beautiful," Ella thought. The most beautiful vault, perhaps, she'd ever seen.

"It just looked so good in the air."

GG's first vault came in at 9.65. It was good enough for a win. The air around the Bees relaxed. Leah smiled. Then GG went for another one.

She rocketed through the air even higher and more perfectly than before, hit her landing, and the room exploded. Maria was so excited that she injured her leg celebrating. (She would spend the rest of the celebration on crutches that had been quickly procured and was checked immediately for a torn Achilles.) The team rushed out and collapsed on GG. A 9.725.

"That," the sophomore thought, "is the title."

GG knew she had it the moment she landed. Of all of the moments in her gymnastics career so far, she said, it was the best. Lea was next, but it didn't matter. She took her turn quickly, knowing it wasn't going to be counted. Brecksville had won. There was no question or waiting for the official score. Lea and Rachel hugged and burst into tears out of a combination of relief and happiness. Despite Rachel's confidence in the back room, they knew how close it was.

"I just feel like the whole year everyone doubted us," Lea said.

"They thought this wasn't the year," Rachel continued. "But we won. That's what was going through my head."

Everyone else in the gym seemed stunned. With the exception of the Brecksville celebration, it was quiet. The final score was Brecksville 148.825, Olentangy Berlin 148.050. Fractions of a point, just like Maria always warned. It was the closest win since 2009 when Brecksville beat Magnificat by 0.125 and the third-highest point total in state history. The streak was safe. Twenty in a row. Ella and Delaney were going to graduate with the streak intact.

"That," said Greg, Maria's brother, as he walked through the groups of parents, coaches, and gymnasts celebrating, "was the wildest meet I've ever been a part of."

Later when the team was driving back to the hotel on the bus, Leah realized the math she had given GG was wrong. She had told her she needed a 9.3 to win.

In fact, GG only needed a 8.95 to tie and a 9.0 to win. She could do that in her sleep. The next day she won the vault event at the individual state meet portion, beating her team score by a tenth of a point.

After the awards ceremony, the team posed for photos on the podium with the trophy and received hugs and congratulations from their parents. Ella stood in the center, taking it all in as her last meet as a Brecksville-Broadview Heights gymnast. She breathed a deep sigh of relief and reflected back on what she was thinking after she landed her vault. "I was just so relieved," she said, "that we weren't going to be the class to break the streak."

A few feet away, Olentangy Berlin's team was gathered in a group, talking to their parents, and figuring out where they were headed next. Jen gave them a quick pep talk. They were sad but also proud to have finished in their team goal: the top three. "We'll be back next year," she told them.

Greg, Maria's brother, came through the room and noticed the two groups. "We should make sure the girls are congratulating Olentangy," he told his sister.

She agreed.

As the Brecksville gymnasts' profile continued to grow, Maria, Leah, and Joan and the rest of the Ganim family worked as hard as they could to make sure they appeared as gracious and sportsmanlike as they could. They instilled in them that everything they do reflected on the program and it's up to them to be as classy as they could be.

Even if it meant congratulating the team that almost ended a (now) twenty-year streak.

. . .

Exhausted and exhilarated, the gymnasts filed back on the bus for the short ride back to the hotel. Before the celebration came tradition. The last entry in "The Fish," the book that was started by the team in 2000 and was passed from gymnast to gymnast after each meet with a note. Delaney, the team captain, read the note she wrote to a freshman, Brooke, who she said impressed her with her energy and effort. The book was passed for the last time that season. And then the celebration began. Lea turned the speaker back on and the music started blasting.

The girls shouted along with DJ Khaled. "Every time I step into a building my hands go up."

Across the bus, the gymnasts all raised their hands and shouted the rest of the words.

"And they stay down."

A thought seemed to suddenly hit Leah and she stood up and looked at her team. "Holy fucking shit," she shouted. "We DID that."

"We had some really good competition, ladies," Maria added. "Some really good competition."

The team cheered and started singing along with Queen's "We Are the Champions."

Joan piped in, bringing back the Black Eyed Peas' song that had gotten their nerves out so many times in the postseason. "And we," she said, "are going to have a good good night."

"Yeah, Ms. G!" one of the gymnasts shouted. The dance party continued.

Sitting in the front of the bus, Maria and Leah had spent most of the bus ride ignoring the celebration while trying to diagnose Maria's calf injury. But Leah stopped to shout out a request.

"Can you turn on my song?" she asked. They obliged and shouted with that one too.

A few songs later, Leah turned back again. "GG," she said. "I still can't believe you stuck that."

GG's response was drowned out by her teammates singing Miley Cyrus's "Party in the U.S.A." Two songs later, the bus driver told them to sit down.

As they neared the hotel, Maria turned her attention away from her injured leg and back to her gymnasts with a request: "My lucky number is twenty-one," she said. "For next year."

Instantly the team DJs went to work and put on the Drake and 21 Savage song with the line "21, can you do somethin' for me?"

Maria laughed and rethought what she had just told the team.

"No," she said, as the trophy sat safely at the back of the bus in Ella's arms.

Next year, she knew she'd have a group of experienced sophomores who had been battle tested as freshmen and understood well now what it takes to win a state title. She knew she'd have a strong group of upperclassmen. She knew that Lea and Jeanne with Rachel, GG, and Emily were a fearsome core. And that next year's team would have more depth: Bailey's ankle would heal; Rachel, a freshman who had been sidelined with shoulder surgery, would be back; Avery would have two years of state competition under her belt.

But she also knew that the competition around her was getting tougher by the year. And that Berlin, Brunswick, and Medina would be coming for them again next year. She knew that Berlin knew they were within arm's reach of beating them—and that they wouldn't forget that feeling.

That could wait, though, she thought, as the team continued to celebrate behind her. "We're going to enjoy this moment," she said. "And savor every second."

It was too late, though. They had gotten the message.

Leah posted a picture of the team posing with the trophy on the team's Instagram page. By the time they had gotten off the bus, the Brecksville gymnasts had each written the same comment: #21canyou dosomethingforme?"

After all, they had a title to defend.

. . .

The second day of the state meet was the individual competition—the gymnasts were in a more club-style competition solo. The excitement of winning the meet on a vault the night before seemed to have helped GG—she hit an even higher score (9.85) to win the individual vault competition.

Tessa, the Padua gymnast who trained with Brecksville, won the state tournament all-around with the second-highest score in Ohio high school gymnastics history—a 38.5. For Leah, it was the icing on the cake. "I didn't really go into that meet expecting to win," Tessa said. "I knew that I was going to have to work for it." But she was feeling good after uneven bars and beam, going into her two strongest events. After vault, her final event, Leah met her with a big hug. "You did it, you won," she told her. "I know it."

Everyone from Brecksville, Padua, and Revere who was at the meet started celebrating. It got emotional. They were all crying and screaming, letting out emotions from not only Tessa's big day but also likely the day before.

Tessa came in second to GG in vault by .25 of a point with a 9.825. That score was tied with Tayten, the Olentangy Berlin freshman. Tayten came in second in the all-around, a reminder that she would be a force to be reckoned with for the next three years. Bree Vargo, a Brunswick gymnast, finished third.

Finally, exhausted, the team climbed into the bus and headed back to Brecksville. They went home and took a nap and then around 9 P.M. went to Ella's house, where the house was stocked with snacks, soda, and rolls and rolls of toilet paper.

There was a problem, though. The usual order of events was that the host parent called the Brecksville police department to let them know that their children were going out toilet papering their friends' houses as part of a long-running and mutually understood tradition.

However, someone in Broadview Heights did not get the memo.

"Broadview Heights police said that they would not allow it without previous permission from the homeowner," Kim, Ella's mom, wrote in the parents' group chat.

But the gymnasts weren't deterred.

The first house they hit was Leah's. They piled into Lea, Ella, and Delaney's cars and Ella's dad Matt followed closely behind to ensure they were safe driving into the city (they did not call the Cleveland Police Department beforehand). At one point, the teenagers stopped for gas, and Matt told Ella that one of the drivers of one of the cars was going too fast and she needed to lead the pack from now on. Driving at a more responsible speed, the group drove into Tremont and found their assistant coach's house.

After last year's toilet papering prank, Leah had had a plan all season to avoid this. She had been considering putting her house on the market and had been incredibly fuzzy on details to the team about the status of that or where she actually lived.

But as she found out, looking through her security cameras that Saturday night, Maria sold her out earlier in the day.

Leah peeked out of her door. This year she was still awake when the gymnasts arrived. The prank wouldn't reach anywhere near the legendary status of last year's.

"You have five minutes," she told the teenagers.

Skunky, the neighbor's skunk they met last year, was nowhere to be found.

The gymnasts got to work, quickly wrapped toilet paper where they could, and dashed back to the car. Tessa Brousek, who joined them for the beloved tradition, proudly watched as even in the few minutes they spent at Leah's, they did considerable damage.

"Her whole backyard, on the power lines, on the deck were draped with toilet paper everywhere, on her garbage cans, on all her bushes. It was everywhere," she said proudly.

Then they hit the houses of the wrestlers, who were away at their state meet. At one of those houses, they were caught by dogs who heard the commotion, causing the gymnasts to race off the property so quickly that some of them fell on the toilet paper. They stopped at Maria's and went to work before being quickly scared off by her husband. Considering their coach's injured calf, they felt a little bad doing too much to her lawn anyway.

Still on an adrenaline high, the team returned to Ella's house around 2 A.M. They stayed up talking until one by one, they fell asleep.

At 10 A.M., Kim reported back to the group chat that she had heard them up and giggling until 5 A.M., but all was quiet.

"Thank you," wrote one of the other moms in the group chat, "for keeping them safe." Kim responded that she was happy to do it. After all, this was the second year that the sleepover hosting fell to her. After this, Ella was done with high school gymnastics and would soon be off to college.

And Kim and Matt were going to miss this too.

A few weeks later, Leah started spreading the word again that she was selling her house. She had no plans to update them with her new address. She really hated cleaning up that toilet paper.

CHAPTER 19

Aftermath

A few weeks after winning the state title, Ella sat in her house in Brecksville, pondering a question. What would have happened if she hadn't hit that vault? She spent her entire high school career with the responsibility of carrying a state title streak and in the three years before, her teammates had been more experienced and provided more of a cushion for her in the state meet. It had been years since a few fractions of a point would have mattered the way they did in that moment where she stood at the state meet temporarily unable to compete a vault she had successfully competed so many times before.

"Right after finding out that we won, I thought back to that moment and just how much pressure was on me at that time and the pressure for all of us throughout the whole meet was just so immense," she said. "A lot of people in high school don't have to go through that pressure and even though it's for sports, it's not something that would ruin your life if it goes wrong, [though] it's still a big deal to keep that streak going."

Maria hoped that all the lessons she had tried to instill in Ella and the rest of the gymnasts would have stuck with her more than anything and helped her move past it, if for some reason she hadn't done that vault. "There is going to be a team that loses and I think the freshmen then wouldn't have been able to experience a state title, but they'd have three more opportunities," she said. "But I knew my seniors had that opportunity to experience it and so many gymnasts or so many athletes don't ever have that opportunity to say they were a state champion of a Division 1 sport in high school. So there's that. And twenty years from now, what are they going to remember? Are they going to remember the relationships they built or that someone fell in state meet? I would never blame it on one individual. So what are they going to remember about that night? Would it be how the team responded together in their relationships that are the most important, or are they going to let it impact the rest of their life because they lost? And hopefully, I've taught them enough for their mental emotional side to be resilient enough to bounce back."

But Ella and Maria didn't have to find out if that's what would have happened.

Throughout the meet, Leah kept reminding herself that they couldn't have done anything differently. Even if they had lost, it wouldn't be because the gymnasts didn't try hard or weren't prepared or weren't performing well. "We had a really good meet," she said. "We really couldn't have done anything differently to change the outcome if we didn't win. And I just think the girls had so much confidence that I couldn't have asked for anything better on their end either to ensure that if we lost, it couldn't have been on them. They didn't have poor attitudes, they weren't, weren't not cheering for each other. They did everything perfect. And if it was our time, it was our time. But the great news is it's not our time."

The team walked in a parade that went from the high school to the middle school, and ended in a bus ride to the elementary school for a celebration. They were honored by the Brecksville City Council and at a Cleveland Cavaliers game. Joan was the grand marshal of the Brecksville Memorial Day parade to honor the team's twentieth consecutive win. She rode in the passenger side of a yellow convertible, top down, waving throughout the parade route.

Maria learned that she partially tore her calf when she was celebrating GG's vault at the state meet. "It's not torn all the way through, but it's torn enough that [the doctor] put me on this, you know, for three weeks," she said, displaying a boot a few weeks later. "It sucks. Truly. I'm supposed to be at Kent State for a reunion tomorrow with my gymnastics friends, and I can't drive. And so one of my teammates is coming to get me, which is totally out of her way."

Bailey, it turned out, was much more injured than initially diagnosed. She had an MRI that showed multiple bone bruises and a nearly torn ligament in her foot. She brushed it off as just another gymnastics injury, continued to rehab it, and began to train for her sophomore season.

For the club gymnasts, the season wasn't over when the high school season ended. Ella ended up competing in the level 9 Eastern Championship.

Both Ella and Delaney graduated and went to college, leaving Lea, Jeanne, and Tessa as the senior leaders for the 2023–24 season as they go for twenty-one in a row. That senior list was missing one important person—Abby, who hit the first vault at the state meet, decided at the start of the school year that she wasn't going to continue on the team for her senior year. "Coach Schneidy and Coach Leah have been hugely supportive of Abby and she will always be thankful of everything she has learned from them. She's moving on to focus on her music and writing and future plans," her mom wrote in the parents' group chat. "We wish the team all of the best this season and will be coming to some meets to cheer the team on!"

For many of the gymnasts who competed for Brecksville, it ended up being something that followed them through their life—whether it's the ability to thrive in high-pressure situations or the former competitors or neighbors who recognized them years later. Some, when they go to college, want to try a whole new identity—one recent alumna said she didn't tell anyone in college that she had competed in high school gymnastics, much less that she was a four-time state champion. Others embraced it as something they'd always loved. And some, like Leah and Alecia, came back to coach at Gym World and hold especially tightly to the thing that they loved the most from an early age—and a family who treated them as their own.

For the Brecksville team, though, the mission remains the same. With the exception of the graduating seniors, the team spent much of the offseason at Gym World, working on upgrades and getting ready for the next season. It's unlikely most of them would compete at the next level and share in the new Name Image Likeness world that overtook college gymnastics. No one was anywhere near a track to make it to the national team. But they hoped they were on track to add to another state title collection. Winning the twentieth consecutive one, as close as it was, did nothing to temper expectations.

In late summer, Leah was looking ahead to the 2023–24 team. "I think the girls are extremely motivated to continue after this past year, and we got a lot of good freshmen coming up, so I'm excited for it. And if they can perform how Emily performed, we'll be in really great hands for this season," she said.

But mostly, she just hoped that, in the end, being on the team would give each of them something to take with them for the rest of their lives—just like it provided for her.

"I just think it was such a crucial and pivotal time in my life," she said.

"I can only hope that the girls that I coach have the feeling that I feel every day—as corny as it is—of being blessed to be a part of that team."

Acknowledgments

This book would not have happened without my dream team of Delia Berrigan and Ashley Smith Becker. I am grateful for their advice, friendship, and most importantly, for them believing in me and this book. I am also grateful to Clara Totten and the team at Kent State University Press.

Special thanks also to Mary Byrne, Leo Simone, Pete Axtman, Chris Korman, Maggie Hendricks, Tania Ganguli, and Maridel Reyes who helped throughout the process and listened to all my anxiety around it endlessly. Greg Presto was the one who said this was a book in the first place (Go Cats), and I'm grateful for his friendship and guidance. Thank you to David Campbell at Cleveland.com for introducing me to the world of OHSAA gymnastics by assigning me my first preview article of the sport right after I moved here. And, of course, thank you to my husband, Randall, who had to listen to me talk endlessly about high school gymnastics for more than two years.

But above all, I am most grateful to Maria, Joan, and the entire Ganim family, Leah Miko, and the Brecksville-Broadview Heights gymnasts past and present and their families for allowing me into their pressure-cooker world, answered my questions patiently, and graciously welcomed me into their homes and their lives without reservation. They were under enough pressure without having someone follow them around and take notes along the way, and I am forever thankful to them for opening their world for a season and beyond to me.

Index

www.ingramcontent.com/pod-product-compliance
Lightning Source LLC
LaVergne TN
LVHW090937080826
845145LV00003B/788

* 9 7 8 1 6 0 6 3 5 5 0 7 7 *